THEORY GYMNASTICS

M000111344

ACCELERANDO·1 — Revised!

Laura Zisette
Charlene Zundel Shelzi
Kathleen Lloyd

kjos

Neil A. Kjos
Music Company

ISBN-10: 0-8497-6383-5
ISBN-13: 978-0-8497-6383-0

Foreword

This Teacher Guide was created as a teacher time-saver. It contains the following:

Cranky Hints from the Three Cranky Women (TCW)
- Suggested group activities for each unit
- A list of TCW games that apply the concepts the students are learning
- Suggested list of listening pages to go along with each unit

Listening List
- Lists of suggested music for student listening by the featured composers

Theory Gymnastics® Answer Key and Listening Resources
- Standard answers for the theory and listening pages
- Ear-training examples for the listening pages

Testing Resources
- Reproducible theory tests (forms A and B) and answer keys
- Ear-training tests (forms A and B) and answer keys
- Ear-training examples to administer the ear-training tests

The Theory Gymnastics® Series
We hope you find the Theory Gymnastics Series to be a fun and motivational vehicle for engaging and challenging your students. We have found this approach to be effective in both individual and group study.

Standard answers are offered for the theory pages in the Theory Gymnastics answer key. However, due to the emphasis on creative thinking, some pages/exercises have more than one possible answer. These pages are noted throughout the guide. To encourage critical thinking, the authors feel that if the student can convincingly defend their answers as an appropriate response, these answers should be considered correct.

Individual Instruction
The units in the theory books are laid out in a progressive order, but may be prescribed in any order to fill an individual student's needs. Teachers may choose to assign pages from units which correspond to the repertoire being studied. The *Practice* pages are worksheets which give students an opportunity to explore the concept. The *Challenge* and *Thinker* pages further reinforce the concept, but are more difficult—and lots of fun!

Listening Pages
Listening pages reinforce concepts studied in the theory section and may reflect concepts studied in a corresponding theory unit. Many students enjoy a short break from the lesson routine to work on listening skills. Some teachers provide comfortable spaces for students to work independently on their listening pages using a portable media player or computer with headphones. Recordings for these listening pages are available online in the Kjos Multimedia Library at www.kjos.com. See page 46 for details.

Group Instruction
The theory books also provide a well-planned curriculum for group theory study. The varying degrees of difficulty found in the *Practice, Challenge,* and *Thinker* pages give the group instructor many teaching options. Because abilities vary among students who are in the same level, the teacher may choose to send early finishers on to the *Challenge* and *Thinker* pages while others in the group are completing the *Practice* pages.

The *Challenge* and *Thinker* pages may also be used as take home or bonus activities. Many students find the *Challenge* and *Thinker* pages to be so enjoyable that the teacher may choose to use these pages as a special incentive. One of the benefits of using theory books in a group situation is the fact that the teacher can easily evaluate each student's level of comprehension.

We do not advocate using only the theory books in group lessons. They are meant to be a resource for teaching music concepts in an organized manner. We do advocate the use of supplementary activities (games, hands-on activities, etc.) for further exploration of the concepts offered in the theory books.

Group classes offer a superb setting for ear training. The teacher has the opportunity to present listening examples to more than one student at a time. The group environment provides students with the opportunity to learn from one another as methods of identifying and reinforcing concepts are discussed.

Reproducible Tests
There are two forms (A and B) of the theory and ear-training tests for each level. Teachers may choose to use one form of the theory test to prepare the students for the final test or as a placement test for new students. The other theory test is useful for testing students at the completion of their theory book to assess their readiness to continue on to the next level. On all tests each question has a point value that is shown in small type to the right of its question. Determine how many points the student has earned for each correct answer (100 possible) and score the tests by adding up these numbers (x/100). The authors use the following guideline for student assessment on the theory test: If students can complete the test with a score of 70% or higher, they can successfully continue on to the next book–with the help of their teacher to strengthen their weak areas. If they receive less than a 70% it may be useful for them to repeat the level, the advantage being that they will become more fluent in the theory they know, and they will be able to fill in the "holes" of the concepts they missed or didn't completely understand, including ear training. (These test scores can be used for the Keyboard Gymnastics® Achievement Program.)

NOTE: Because the theory and ear-training tests are reproducible and can potentially be administered to many students over a period of years, it will be important to take steps to preserve their integrity. For example, do not send tests home with students. Administer tests in an environment where proper precautions can be taken in the distribution and gathering of the test. **The theory and ear-training test answer keys and ear-training test examples may not be duplicated.**

Our Objective
Our objective is to always put the students' needs first as we nurture them along in their musical experience. However, as teachers we know what a boon it is to have resources and materials that work for us and for our students! Enjoy!

The Three Cranky Women,
Laura, Kathleen and Charlene

Laura, Kathleen and Charlene

Supporting Material for

ACCELERANDO 1

TEACHER AIDS

◇ **Student Flashcards** (TW430) ★

◇ **Teacher Flashcards** (TW530)

◇ **Music Money** (TW540) ★

◇ **Kreative Keyboard**® (TW605)
Cloth keyboard and grand staff

◇ **Kreative Keyboard**® **Collection** (TW604)
Book of 24 games

◇ **Kreative Keyboard**® **Game Materials** (TW607)
Reproducible game props

GAMES

◇ **Beat This!** (TW615) ★

◇ **Slap Me Silly** (TW611)

◇ **Note Nabber** (TW620) ★

◇ **Tapping Telephones**® (TW601) ★
Levels A and B

◇ **Flashy Fingers** (TW616)

◇ **Rockin' Rhythms** (TW617A)
Beginning and Elementary levels

◇ **Wacky Words** (TW614A) ★
Starring Wanda

◇ **Wacky Words** (TW614B) ★
Starring Walter

◇ **Musical Spoons**®–**Notes** (TW602A) ★

◇ **Musical Spoons**®–**Triads** (TW602C) ★

◇ **Screamin' Match** (TW610) ★
Elementary level cards only

◇ **Scale Scramble**® (TW603) ★

◇ **Nifty Notes** (TW550)

◇ **Perfect One** (TW613)

◇ **Music Blitz** (TW612)

★ *Available in revised version.*

All above materials available from Neil A. Kjos Music Company
www.kjos.com

Contents

Tests Form A:

Tests Form B:

Cranky Hints for Teaching Group Classes

1. Discuss class rules at the first class such as:

   - Bring all your materials each time (including a pencil).

   - Have your homework done each time you come to class.

   - No chewing gum.

   - No talking while the teacher explains something.

   - No noisy or distracting electronic devices are allowed in class.

   In our experience, we have found that if students participate in setting the rules for the class, they tend to keep those rules. It helps to limit the number of rules and keep the wording brief. You might consider having the students set a consequence for breaking each rule and/or a class reward for keeping the rules. For example, students who did not bring back finished work must finish it during game time. However, we prefer to use the positive approach whenever possible. (e.g., **Rule:** All students who come to class with finished theory homework can participate in theory games while the other students finish their homework in class.)

2. Teach the students the definition and pronunciation of the name of their theory book. (You can find this information on the Foreword page of the theory book.)

3. Group class can be structured in as many different ways as there are teachers. We have found the following "formula" to be very effective, yet flexible:

   - Review last week's assignment. This could include correcting pages.

   - Play a game to review the concept introduced the previous week, or any concept that needs reinforcement or review.

   - Practicing ear-training that corresponds with the theory being worked on can be a great learning tool. (See suggested ear-training exercises for each unit in the pages that follow.)

   - Introduce and discuss the new concept.

   - Conduct an activity using the new concept.

   - Play a game to reinforce the new concept.

   - Assign *Practice* pages. Have the students begin working on them during class time so any questions may be addressed before they leave.

   - Look ahead to the *Challenge* and *Thinker* pages with your students for anything that may need clarification. (This also gets the students excited to go on to these pages.)

4. When introducing a new concept, read the *Discovery* pages together with your students so you can "discover" what they do and do not understand before they go home to work on the *Practice*, *Challenge*, and *Thinker* pages.

5. Giving out Music Money (TW540) freely for good behaviors such as correct answers, being on time, good teamwork, winning games, etc. can work wonders. Give short quizzes for those who are on time to earn music money. Earned music money can be "spent" in many ways: periodically have items for purchase such as soda, movie tickets, or anything that motivates the students. Have an auction and let them bid for items. Teens really enjoy the competitive nature of the auction. Have fun!

6. Speaking of fun . . . the "fun factor" can be simple, but make a big difference. For example, when they hear "go," students playing a speed game could be required to yell the music alphabet backward before leaving their position. Maybe they have to finish chewing and swallowing a marshmallow before yelling the music alphabet and finishing the rest of the race requirements. If they are slapping an answer (card), they could be required to start with their hands on their head, or sitting on their hands. A step could be added to the race in which the student must play the note, interval, five-finger pattern, or chord on the piano before they draw it on a board – and then you could keep adding steps with the students' input. The fun factor could be something as simple as having them choose team names that are in line with a theme (for example, composers or sports) or create a riddle that the other team has to solve. They could be earning points that give them "super-hero powers" – powers that could then be used as a crossover to another activity or for immunity in the game. Anything that adds some interest, fun, or silliness to an activity is sure to keep students engaged. The fun factor is only limited by the imagination.

Cranky Hints for each Unit in
Accelerando 1

Unit 1: The Music Alphabet & Notes on the Keyboard

Activity 1: Use the back of the *Wacky Words* (starring Wanda) cards and spell the words with markers (such as tokens or pieces of candy) on the *Kreative Keyboard®*.

Activity 2: Use two *Kreative Keyboards®* and have two students mark the same white key on their keyboard (e.g., "C"). Shout out a number, a direction (ascending or descending) and the word "steps" or "skips." For example, if the teacher calls out "Five descending steps!", the students race to be the first to say "C–B–A–G–F" and place a marker on the final key (in this case F). As another example, if the students begin on "A" and the teacher calls out "Four ascending skips!", the student who calls out "A-C-E-G" and places a marker on "G" wins. Award Music Money for each correct answer.

Specific Page Suggestion: Accelerando 1, p. 7 – Work through the first few elements of each exercise together to make sure the students understand what is required.

Suggested Games: *Music Blitz.* Remove all the cards with flats and sharps leaving only the A, B, C, D, E, F and G cards. Play as usual except spell the music alphabet instead of scales in the center of the playing area. After the students are proficient at spelling A to G, have them spell E to D, B to A, etc. For an extra challenge, have the students try spelling the music alphabet backward.

Listening Unit 20: page 131A "Same or Different Pitch"; page 131B "Same or Different Melody"

Unit 2: The Grand Staff

Activity: Seat the students in a circle. Explain how to draw the grand staff. Give each student a piece of paper and a different color of pencil. Each student, in turn, draws one part of the grand staff and passes it on to the next student. Give students Music Money for each part of the staff they draw correctly.

Suggested Games: *Screamin' Match, Slap Me Silly*

Listening Unit 20: page 132A "High or Low"; page 132B "Loud or Soft"; page 134A "Crescendo or Decrescendo (Diminuendo)"; page 134B "Ascending or Descending"

Unit 3: Note Values and Time Signatures

Activity 1: Separate the quarter note, half note, dotted half note, and whole note cards from the *Screamin' Match* deck. Use these cards to play *Memory.* Shuffle the cards and place them face down in even rows. Students take turns flipping over two cards. If they find a matchAward Music Money for each match after all the cards have been matched.

Activity 2: Use the rhythm cards and wizard cards from *Beat This!* that have quarter, half, dotted half, and whole notes. Place the wizard cards **face down** in one stack and the note cards **face down** in a stack beside them. Each student takes turns drawing one card from each stack and performing the rhythms in the different and fun ways according to the instructions on the wizard cards.

Specific Page Suggestion: Accelerando 1, p. 19A, B, C – Work through this page as a class. Clap and count the rhythms together with the students, then clap each rhythm incorrectly and have the students identify the mistakes.

Suggested Games: *Rockin' Rhythms* (Beginning), *Tapping Telephones®* (Level A)

Listening Unit 20: page 133A "Slow or Fast"; page 133B "Steady or Unsteady"

Unit 4: The Guideposts

Activity 1: Have students help you extract the guidepost cards from the Teacher Flashcards (TW530) deck. Divide the class into two teams. Place the guidepost flashcards face down. Show one guidepost flashcard to one student from each team. Then have these students take turns describing the guidepost note on the card to his/her teammates using one-word clues without naming the note. For example, a high C note is shown. The student from team one might say "high," the student from team two might follow by saying, "ledger" or "second" (for second ledger line), etc. The first team to correctly identify the guidepost wins a point. For the next note, the student from team two gets to go first, and so on. When there is only one guidepost card left, the student who can identify it (without turning it over) wins an extra point for their team.

Activity 2: Use the *Musical Spoons®–Notes* cards to play Memory or Go Fish with only the cards that picture guidepost notes on the keyboard and staff.

Activity 3: Divide the class into two teams. Use only the guidepost note cards from the Student Flashcards (TW430). Shuffle the cards and place them in a stack on the piano rack. One student from each team races to be the first to say and play the guideposts on the piano as the teacher reveals them one at a time. **Note:** Play two rounds—one with the "note name" side of the card and one with the "note on the staff" side of the card. *Variation:* Show the name side of a flashcard to the first two players from each team. When you say "go" the two students race to the board to be the first to draw the correct note. The game continues with the next player from each team. Award one point for each note that is drawn correctly.

Activity 4: Play "Mirror Image." This activity works well if you have a small group (up to 6). Divide the class into two teams. The first player from each team is shown a note name and then races to the board to draw the note on the grand staff, then races back to tag the next student. The second student then races to the board to draw and label the 'mirror' or symmetrical note for that guidepost. For example, F above middle C is shown to the first students. These students run to the board to draw it, then run back and tag the second student on their team. That student races up to the board, draws and labels the "Mirror Image" (the symmetrical or inverted guidepost note which in this case would be the G below Middle C) and races back to his team. The first of the two players to slap the hand of their teammate wins one point for their team.

Specific Page Suggestion: Accelerando 1, p. 26 – Describe one of the guidepost notes to the class. Have each student use their own set of Student Flashcards to find and display the note that was described.

Suggested Games: *Musical Spoons®–Notes, Slap Me Silly, Kreative Keyboard*—"What's Your Line or Space?"

Listening Unit 20: page 134C "Ascending or Descending/Crescendo or Decrescendo"

Unit 5: The Notes Between the Guideposts

Activity 1: Use the Teacher Flashcards to play "Electricity." Divide students into two groups. Have each group sit on the floor in a line with their backs to the teacher. Sit at the head of the two lines so that their backs are facing you. (A student can fill your role if there are an odd number of students.) Ask the first student at the head of each line to turn and face you, then have each line clasp their hands together. Before showing the flashcards to these two students, announce the note they are looking for. (e.g., When you say "B," the students will be looking for a "B" in any octave.) As soon as the specified note comes up, the first student of each group quickly squeezes the hand of the next student, then the next, then the next, until the "electrical impulse" travels all the way through the line. The first player at the end of the 'electrical' line to shout (or ring a bell, beat a drum, tap a triangle . . . whatever you might choose) scores a point for their team. Students shift positions so that two new students are "up." Shuffle the flashcards, call out a new note, and resume play. If an electrical impulse is sent down a line at the wrong time, one point is deducted from the team score.

Activity 2: Use the Teacher Flashcards to play *Around the World.* Have students sit in a circle. Choose one student to go and stand behind another student. The student standing is "it." The teacher displays a flashcard and the two students (one standing and the seated student in front of him/her) race to identify the note on a flashcard. If the student who is "it" is the first to identify the note, he or she moves on to the next student, trying to make it all the way around the circle to win. If the student sitting down identifies the card first, he or she becomes "it" and moves on to the next student and tries to continue around the circle. Continue until one student successfully makes it around the world (around the circle).

Specific Page Suggestions: Accelerando 1, pp. 33-35 – Students race to be the first to complete these exercises. Time the students and have them write their time in the squares provided on each page. Score 1 point for each correctly identified note. Students should add up the times as they go. The student with the fastest time is awarded 10 points. All students that finish add 5 points to their score. Determine a winner after all three pages have been completed.

Suggested Games: *Kreative Keyboard*®–Legendary Ledgers, *Musical Spoons*®–Notes, *Note Nabber*, *Nifty Notes*–Quarter Note Football, *Wacky Words (Wanda & Walter)*.

Listening Unit 21: page 149 "Do-Re-Mi-Fa-Sol"

Unit 6: Flats, Sharps, and Naturals

Activity 1: Use the *Kreative Keyboard*® to practice locating sharps and flats on the keyboard, and placing sharps and flats before notes on the staff. Emphasize the exact placement of sharps and flats on the same line or space as the note.

Activity 2: Supply blank 3 x 5 cards and have the students write both names of each piano key that has two names: C, B♯, C♯,D♭, D♯, E♭, E, F♭,F, E♯, F♯, G♭, G♯, A♭, A♯, B♭, B, C♭. The result is one deck of 18 cards. Sit the students in a circle and shuffle the cards. Place the top card face up in the center of the playing area. Continue placing cards one at a time in a line in the playing area. When an enharmonic pair shows up, the players race to grab the two cards as a match. Players keep the matches they have grabbed. Continue playing until all the cards have been matched. Now line up the students at the piano–most matches to least. The student with the most matches goes first and plays their matches (enharmonic notes) on the piano. Incorrectly played matches are surrendered to the next player and so on down the line until all the matches have been played. Points or Music Money may be awarded for correctly played matches.

Specific Page Suggestion: Accelerando 1, p. 42 – Turn this page into a race.

Suggested Games: *Kreative Keyboard*®–Easy Enharmonics.

Listening Unit 21: page 150A & B "More Singing with Solfeggio"

Unit 7: Steps and Skips, Half Steps and Whole Steps

Activity: After discussing half and whole steps, have the students sit in a circle. Demonstrate to the students a simple quarter-note rhythm to clap: Pat (on knees)—Pat (on knees)—Clap (hands)—Snap (fingers). This rhythm continues as the game is played. Announce the name of a note on the "snap" and the student to the left says the name of the note that is a half step up on the next "snap". The students continue around the circle saying the name of the next note a half step up when their fingers "snap". Change to half step down when a mistake is made or when you get back to the note name on which you began. Also try whole step up and whole step down. Then combine (alternate) whole and half steps up, and whole and half steps down.

Specific Page Suggestion: Accelerando 1, p. 45D – Do one of the shapes (circle, square or triangle) at a time. Suggest that the students plan ahead by considering the three possible answers for each shape. Use a different color for each shape.

Specific Page Suggestion: Accelerando 1, p. 47C – Remind students that when they are counting whole and half steps, do not include the key they are already on.

Suggested Games: *Slap Me Silly*

Listening Unit 20: page 135A "Steps or Skips"; page 135B "Steps or Skips/Crescendo or Decrescendo"

Unit 8: Intervals—Unisons through Octaves

Activity: Tell the students that you are going to describe intervals to them and that they are only to consider the white keys of the piano for their answers. Question students: "What is the 4th note up from A?" (They should answer "D.") Then say, "From A to D is a 4th." Continue questioning in this manner until the students understand the concept.

Suggested Games: *Perfect One*, *Slap Me Silly*, *Kreative Keyboard*®—Intellectual intervals, What's Your Line or Space?, Interval Investigators, In-Tune Intervals

Note: Now is a great time to discuss the "sound" of each of these intervals by introducing the folk songs that begin with the intervals (see page 141 in the student theory book). Students should learn to sing the first two notes of these songs beginning on any pitch.

Listening Unit 20: page 138B "Thinking of a Song"; page 139A "Perfect Intervals, Basic Level"; page 140 "Two More Major Intervals"

Unit 9: Review #1

Activity 1: Flashcard drills – Have students drill each other on their Student Flashcards. Students should keep track of missed notes by placing those cards in a separate stack as they go. Put all the "missed notes" cards together for a final class note drill, but first have each pair of students memorize or write down the notes in their pile of missed note cards so they can retrieve their cards after the final class note drill.

Activity 2: Use the *Note Nabber* note-on-the-staff cards and deal seven cards to each player. These cards are placed face up in front of each player. The students race to build common piles of the notes A through G (in any clef) in the center of the playing area. The first player to use all their cards wins.

Note: Many of the activities suggested for Units 4 and 5 are also useful here.

Specific Page Suggestions: Accelerando 1, pp. 54-55 – Give students time to mentally name all the notes on each line first. Then time the students as they see how fast they can complete each problem.

Suggested Games: *Musical Spoons®–Notes, Note Nabber, Slap Me Silly, Wacky Words (Wanda & Walter), Nifty Notes*–Quarter Note Football (students who receive 21 points are awarded the "game ball" quarter), *Perfect One.*

Listening Unit 20: page 139B "Perfect Intervals, Challenge Level"; page 140A "Just the Major Intervals, Please, Basic Level"

Unit 10: Major Five-Finger Patterns and I Chords on the Keyboard

Activity 1: Using the four decks in the *Music Blitz* game, give each student or pairs/teams of students a deck. Have the students race to spell the five-finger patterns in a specified amount of time, one group at a time. Give out Music Money for each correct answer.

Activity 2: Play "The Hot Seat." Each student takes a turn sitting in the "Hot Seat." The teacher has a big mixed bag of four types of sandwich cookies: all vanilla, all chocolate, vanilla with chocolate filling, chocolate with vanilla filling. Explain to the students that each type of cookie represents a I chord group. In this case, the all chocolate cookie represents the oddball group. When the teacher pulls out a cookie, the student in the "hot seat" has to name a corresponding I chord before the teacher (or the class) can count "3, 2, 1." If the student beats the "clock," they earn their cookie.

Activity 3: Play "Musical Sets." Using the *Music Blitz* cards, lay out the top 16 cards of the shuffled deck in even rows (4 cards horizontal x 4 cards vertical). Students gather around the cards and try to find and grab a "set" (three cards that spell a major I chord) before the other students. The card "feeder" (usually the teacher) will keep the blank spots filled in with cards from the deck. The student or team that gathers the most "sets" wins.

Specific Page Suggestions: Accelerando 1, Unit 10 – Read through the Discovery pages (pages 59-61) as a class.

Note: It is important to dedicate enough time to this unit to be sure students feel secure in their knowledge of major five-finger patterns. Frequent reviews throughout out the year are highly recommended.

Suggested Games: *Flashy Fingers, Scale Scramble®, Music Blitz* (spell five-finger patterns instead of scales), Spoons using the *Flashy Fingers* deck, *Kreative Keyboard®*—Fabulous Five, Five-Finger Frenzy

Listening Units 20 and 21: page 139C "Perfect Intervals, Genius Level"; page 140B "Just the Major Intervals, Please, Challenge Level"; page 150C "Solfeggio Dictation"

Unit 11: Major Five-Finger Patterns and I Chords on the Staff

Activity 1: Students practice visualizing the notes of the I chords on the keyboard with this activity. Use two colors of flat, round markers (plastic game chips or white and black buttons, for example). The teacher places one color of marker on the staff side of the **Kreative Keyboard®** to represent the three notes in a I chord. The teacher gives the other color of markers to one of the students and they place their markers on top of the notes of the I chord to mark the notes that are played on the black keys of the piano. Continue until the teacher has all twelve I chords have been placed (one at a time) on the staff. Do the same with the five-finger patterns.

Activity 2: Give one color of **Music Blitz** cards to each student or team. Each team sits on the floor with their backs toward the other team(s). When you say "GO" each student/team spells as many major five-finger patterns and I chords with their deck of **Blitz** cards as they can by placing them face up on the floor. Time the students for one minute. When time is up, compare the patterns and chords that have been spelled. Eliminate all the duplicates and score one point for each of the correct five-finger patterns and I chords that are unique to each student/team. Continue as outlined for five rounds.

Specific Page Suggestion: Accelerando 1, p. 71 – Remind the students how to draw and place accidentals on the staff when multiple accidentals are needed with chords.

Suggested Games: *Kreative Keyboard*–Five-Finger Frenzy, The Fabulous Five, Tasty Triads, Tic–Tac Triads, Trivial Triads.

Listening Unit 20: page 137 "Intervals in a Major Five-Finger Pattern"; page 138A "Using the Five-Finger Pattern"; page 141C "Just the Major Intervals, Genius Level"

Unit 12: Rhythm–Eighth Notes and Rests; Dotted Quarter Notes

Activity 1: Use Hershey® chocolate bars to visually reinforce the concept of eighth notes. Use a Hershey® bar that is sectioned into 12 pieces. Break off 4 pieces from each bar and give 8 pieces to each student on a small paper plate (either in a block of 8 pieces or two blocks of 4 pieces).

Demonstrate the dividing of beats by placing one 8-piece block of candy into a "measure" to equal a whole note. Break that piece into two 4-piece blocks to demonstrate two half notes in a whole note. Break one of the 4-piece blocks into two 2-piece blocks to demonstrate two quarter notes in a half note. Finally break one of the 2-piece blocks into two 1-piece blocks to demonstrate two eighth notes in a quarter note.

Direct the students to break their "whole note" bars into two half notes, then break one of the "half note" bars into two "quarter notes," then break one of the "quarter note" bars into two "eighth notes."

Ask the students how many single pieces (eighth notes) would be in a dotted half note and demonstrate with your 4-piece "half note" plus one 2-piece "quarter note."

Don't eat the candy yet! Have the students make two measures in $\frac{2}{4}$ time represented by their chocolate bar pieces. When they can clap and count their chocolate rhythm correctly, they can eat their chocolate bar.

Activity 2: Use Hershey® chocolate bars to make dotted quarter-eighth rhythms. Use three sections of chocolate to represent the dotted quarter note, and one section to represent the eighth note. Give each student eight sections of chocolate bar and instruct them to plan out one measure of $\frac{4}{4}$ time, then break their bar apart to construct that rhythm out of the chocolate sections. They must use at least one dotted quarter-eighth rhythm.

Activity 3: One of the best ways we have found to reinforce rhythm and counting is to have the students play *War* using the **Beat This!** cards. Have the students count using eighth beats. (See the description for this activity in the **Beat This!** instruction cards.)

Specific Page Suggestion: Accelerando 1, p. 76 – Divide the class into two teams. Each team claps and counts the rhythms together as a team while maintaining a steady beat. The teams are rewarded with Music Money. If they clap it perfectly on the first try, they earn $10 for each team member; second try, $5 each; and third try, $3 each.

Suggested Games: *Beat This!, Rockin' Rhythms* (Elementary), *Tapping Telephones®* (Level B), *Kreative Keyboard®*–Rad Rhythms

Listening Unit 20: page 141 "All the Intervals"; page 143 "Same or Different Rhythm"; page 144A "Will the Real Rhythm Please Stand Up?"

Unit 13: Review #2

Specific Page Suggestion: Accelerando 1, p. 82 – Work this page in pencil first.

Suggested Games: *Scale Scramble®, Beat This!, Rockin' Rhythms* (Elementary), *Flashy Fingers, Tapping Telephones®* (Level A), *Musical Spoons®–Triads*

Listening Unit 20: page 144B "Will the Real Rhythm Please Stand Up?"; page 145A & B "Rhythmic Dictation #1"

Unit 14: Minor Five-Finger Patterns and i Chords

Activity: Using the cards from *Music Blitz*, have the students spell a major five-finger pattern, then remove the 3rd and replace it with the "lowered 3rd" note card. Reinforce the concept that a lowered 3rd for a sharped note becomes a natural, and a natural becomes a flat. (There are no double flats in this book.) Continue spelling Major/minor five-finger patterns until the students understand the concept, then spell minor five-finger patterns without first spelling the major. Do the same with Major and minor I/i chords.

Note: Some suggested activities for Units 10 and 11 may also work well for this unit.

Specific Page Suggestion: Accelerando 1, p. 89 – Remind students that each row and each column must contain numbers 1 through 6.

Specific Page Suggestion: Accelerando 1, p. 91 – Choose "Real-Life Enharmonics" as a class and reward students for creativity with Music Money.

Specific Page Suggestion: Accelerando 1, p. 93 – Remind students that five-finger patterns may span more than one measure. Descending patterns may be hard to see.

Suggested Games: *Scale Scramble®, Music Blitz, Musical Spoons®–Triads, Kreative Keyboard—* Five Finger Frenzy, Tasty Triads, Tic-Tac Triads, Trivial Triads, Minor Madness, What's Your Line or Space?

Listening Unit 20: 136A "Major or Minor Five-Finger Pattern"; page 146A "Rhythmic Dictation #2"

Unit 15: Major and Minor Thirds and Triads

Activity 1: Have the students bring their lesson and/or repertoire books to class. Divide the class into two teams. Each team analyzes the music they brought for one minute, keeping track of each major and minor triad (blocked or broken) that they find. The members of the team that identify the most chords in the specified amount of time are awarded 5 points each.

Activity 2: Triad Exit Quiz. Use questions, such as those below, to ask the students before they are permitted to exit class. A treat may be the reward for the correct answer.

Triad Quiz:

    1. This major triad has "G" as its root. Spell it: _____ _____ _____

    2. This major triad has "E" as its fifth. Spell it: _____ _____ _____

    3. This minor triad has "A" as its third. Spell it: _____ _____ _____

    4. This major triad has "B" as its fifth. Spell it: _____ _____ _____

    5. This minor triad has "Eb" as its third. Spell it: _____ _____ _____

Activity 3: Play "Name my Triad." Each student thinks of a triad and how to spell it. One student is chosen to go first and stands in front of the class. After whispering their triad's name in the teacher's ear they proceed to describe it to the class in this order:

    1. My triad is major (or minor).

    2. Its 3rd is _____.

    3. Its 5th is _____.

    4. Its root is _____.

The first student to yell out the complete name of the triad and spell the triad (e.g., A♭ Major – A♭-C-E♭) is awarded Music Money and is the next to describe their triad. The student describing the triad is also awarded Music Money if they spelled the triad correctly. The more triads a student successfully identifies, the more chances they will have to describe other triads to the class – and earn more Music Money.

Specific Page Suggestions: Accelerando 1, p. 101 – Reinforce the correct placement of accidentals beside each chord. (Also refer back to p. 71 in the theory book.)

Suggested Games: *Musical Spoons®–Triads, Kreative Keyboard–*Trivial Triads, Tasty Triads, Tic-Tac Triads, What's Your Line or Space?

Listening Unit 20: 136B "Major or Minor Third"; 136C "Major or Minor I (i) Chord; page 146B "Rhythmic Dictation #2"

Unit 16: Terms and Signs

Activity: Play *Hangman* with the terms and signs in this unit to reinforce spelling. The student must be able to define the term for the answer to be considered correct. As a fun additional challenge, play again using the scrambled version of the terms found on page 108.

Specific Page Suggestion: Accelerando 1, p. 109 – Work through the story together as a class.

Specific Page Suggestion: Accelerando 1, p. 111 – Answers will vary. As long as the students can satisfactorily defend their answers, consider them correct. For an extra fun challenge, play with the scrambled version of the terms on page 108.

Suggested Games: *Screamin' Match*

Listening Unit 20: 132C "High or Low/Loud or Soft" page 133C; "Slow or Fast/Steady or Unsteady"

Unit 17: Composition - Rhythm

Specific Page Suggestion: Accelerando 1, pp. 112-113 – Be sure to read through the Discovery pages with the students.

Specific Page Suggestion: Accelerando 1, pp. 114-116 – While clapping or tapping a steady beat, have the student(s) say the words to your beat, and then help them figure out what rhythm they created. Have them say the words more than one way and then choose their favorite. Keep an open mind and be very encouraging as the students figure out rhythms to go with the poems. To give the students more experience and practice with this concept, think of other ideas for which students can create rhythms, such as student's names, or a phrase such as "I love to play Ultimate Frisbee®."

Suggested Game: *Tapping Telephones®* (Level A)

Listening Unit 20: page 142A "Major and Perfect Intervals"; page 147A "Rhythmic Dictation #3"

Unit 18: Composition - Melody

Activity: Show the class simple songs that use repetition and sequence in their melodies (e.g., "Three Blind Mice," "Row, Row, Row Your Boat," "Peter, Peter Pumpkin Eater," "Heart and Soul") Then create (or have a student create) a simple pattern at the piano and have a student(s) use it to create a sequence and a repetition at the piano.

Note: This is a great unit to use for Halloween. It is easier to compose music when students can create musical pictures. Consider the age level of your students for this activity when choosing imagery. Younger students might respond well to words such as "funny," "crazy," "unhappy witch," or "troll." Ask older students to create a musical ambience similar to movie music. Use words such as "dark," "sad," "upset," "emotional," "thriller," or "mysterious." After the students compose their pieces, you may wish to hold a composition recital. Halloween composition recitals are especially fun where students can dress in costumes to match their composition. Consider creating a book for each student that includes every composition of the recital.

Note: Some ways to make a composition sound "scary": use a minor five-finger pattern, include the augmented 4th interval, use a whole-tone scale, include sudden dynamic changes.

Specific Page Suggestion: Accelerando 1, pp. 117-118 – You may wish to create a poster with the ten "Steps for Composing a Melody." (Or you can simply write the steps on the board.)

Specific Page Suggestion: Accelerando 1, p. 121 – It can be fun to write a four-line poem as a class and have everyone choose a rhythm and notes to go with it. Compare the compositions and point out their similarities and differences and how the students did or did not follow the "Ten Steps for Composing a Melody." See rhythm suggestions found on pages 114-116 of the theory book.

Listening Units 20 and 21: 142B "Major and Perfect Intervals"; page 147B "Rhythmic Dictation #3"; 151 "Solfeggio in Harmony"

Unit 19: Review #3

Specific Page Suggestion: Accelerando 1, p. 130 – Help the students find a few of the items in the music before they begin to analyze on their own.

Suggested Games: *Scale Scramble*® (with five-finger patterns), *Musical Spoons*®–*Triads*, *Tapping Telephones*® (Levels A and B), *Flashy Fingers, Perfect One* (without the M6, M7, and P8 cards)

Listening Units 20 and 21: 142C "Major and Perfect Intervals"; page 148 "Rhythmic Dictation #4"; 152A & B "Where's the Do?"

Unit 20: Listening

You may use the pages in this unit more than once by having the students mark their answers with a different color each time they do a page. (This will require making up different listening examples for each page or playing the given examples in a different order each time.) Use these exercises along with the other units as the student progresses through Accelerando 1.

Activity 1: Use the *Perfect One* cards. Play as usual, but each time a card is played, the student who played it must sing the interval or take back their card (if sung incorrectly).

Activity 2: *Rockin' Rhythms* – Clap the rhythms on the cards to the students. Have students take turns trying to clap and count the rhythm from memory. Reward the first student to clap and count the rhythm back correctly with Music Money. (This may require the teacher to clap and count the rhythm more than once.)

Specific Page Suggestion: Accelerando 1, pp. 143-148 – Count off the eighth notes before you begin to clap and count each rhythm.

Unit 21: Solfeggio

Activity: Use the *Kreative Keyboard* and five flat, round markers (game pieces or pennies also work) to reinforce "Do-Re-Mi-Fa-Sol" on the staff. Sing them as a group—first as "1-2-3-4-5" and then as "Do-Re-Mi-Fa-Sol." Have the students mix up the five markers and then sing them as a group (always begin on "Do").

Specific Page Suggestion: Accelerando 1, pp. 149, 150, 152 – Sing these pages as a class.

Specific Page Suggestion: Accelerando 1, pp. 151 – Sing only the melody or harmony parts with your partner before you try to sing it as a duet.

Teacher Note: Offer to pay Music Money to students who bring and sing one of their lesson book melodies using solfeggio.

Unit 22:

Mozart

Activity: Have the students read the whole story of Mozart and write down at least one fact from each paragraph. Divide the class into two teams. One student from team one draws a picture of one of their facts on the chalkboard. The rest of their team has 30 seconds to identify the fact that the student has drawn. If they are successful, the team is awarded one point. Continue with team two drawing a Mozart fact. After a fact has been drawn and identified, it may not be used again. Continue until all the facts the students have written have been identified. **Note:** You will need to combine paragraphs 1 & 2 and 6 & 7 of the Mozart story.

Specific Page Suggestion: Accelerando 1, p. 155 – There are many answers to this page. If the student can convincingly argue why they chose to mark the sections as they did, it is considered correct. Award Music Money for each correctly identified repetition and sequence.

Beethoven

Activity: Give an answer (for example: "He was known for being able to play the piano blindfolded"), and have students respond with either "Who is Mozart?" or "Who is Beethoven?" ("Who is Mozart?" would be correct for the above answer.) To mix it up a little, add a third component using student's names or even yours: "She is know for having performed in the Monster Concert five times." "Who is Sally?" or, "He not only drew notes accurately, but he could chew a marshmallow faster than any other classroom musician." "Who is Rudy?" We suggest that these inserts should be treated like cooking with jalapeno peppers – don't add too many!

Specific Page Suggestions: Accelerando 1, p. 158 – Look over the timeline events before reading the story. Have the class fill in the missing events as you read.

Specific Page Suggestions: Accelerando 1, p. 159 – Play a recording of *Für Elise* for the students before they reconstruct the theme.

Music Listening List of Works by Wolfgang Amadeus Mozart:

1. Minuet in F Major (for piano), K2
2. The Marriage of Figaro K492, Overture
3. Piano Sonata in A Major, K331, 3rd Movement ("Rondo Alla Turca")
4. Eine Kleine Nachtmusik, K525
5. Piano Sonata in A Major, K331, 1st Movement (Theme and Variations)
6. Requiem in D Minor K626, Confutatis Maledictis
7. Fantasie in C Minor (for piano), K475
8. Piano Sonata in C Major, K545, 3rd Movement (Rondo)

Music Listening List of Works by Ludwig van Beethoven:

1. Für Elise (for piano), WoO 59
2. Symphony No. 5 in C Minor, Op. 67, 1st Movement
3. Piano Sonata in C Minor, Op. 13 ("Pathetique"), all movements
4. Quartet in C for Piano & String Trio, WoO 36, No. 3, 3rd Movement
5. Piano Concerto No. 5 in Eb Major, Op. 73 ("The Emperor")
6. Piano Sonata in C# Minor, Op. 27, No. 2 ("Moonlight"), 1st Movement
7. Ruins of Athens, Op. 113, No. 4 ("Turkish March")
8. Symphony No. 9, Op. 125, 4th Movement-coda

UP AND DOWN, FORWARD AND BACKWARD

A.

1. Write the music alphabet on the keyboard below. Begin on the lowest **A** and move *up*.

A B C D E F G A B C D E F G A B

C D E F G A B C

The music alphabet doesn't always begin on A. Sometimes it begins on another letter. This music alphabet begins on *C* and ends on *C*.

C D E F G A B C D E F G A B

2. Now write the music alphabet backward. Begin on the highest **B** and move *down*.

B. Finish writing the following music alphabets:

Begin here ➝ **1.** F G A B C D E F

Begin here ➝ **2.** G A B C D E F G

3. A B C D E F G A ← Begin here

C. Fill in the missing letters of these music alphabets *moving forward*:

Begin here ➝ **1.** B C D E F G A B

Begin here ➝ **2.** D E F G A B C D

D. Fill in the missing letters of these music alphabets *moving backward*:

1. C D E F G A B C ← Begin here

2. E F G A B C D E ← Begin here

THREE LAME EXCUSES FOR NOT PRACTICING

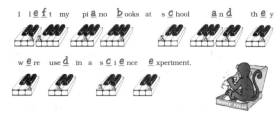

Discover the lame excuses for not practicing by filling in each blank with the name of the note marked on the keyboard.

Excuse #1:

I l <u>e</u> <u>f</u> t my pi <u>a</u> no <u>b</u> ooks at s <u>c</u> hool <u>a</u> n <u>d</u> th <u>e</u> y

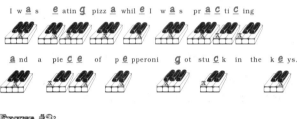

w <u>e</u> re use <u>d</u> in a s <u>c</u> i <u>e</u> nce <u>e</u> xperiment.

Excuse #2:

I w <u>a</u> s <u>e</u> atin <u>g</u> pizz <u>a</u> whil <u>e</u> I w <u>a</u> s pr <u>a</u> <u>c</u> ti <u>c</u> ing

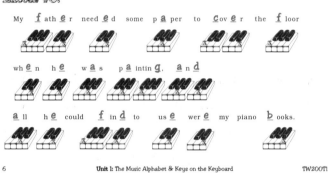

<u>a</u> nd a pie <u>c</u> <u>e</u> of p <u>e</u> pperoni <u>g</u> ot stu <u>c</u> k in the k <u>e</u> ys.

Excuse #3:

My <u>f</u> ath <u>e</u> r need <u>e</u> d some p <u>a</u> per to <u>C</u> ov <u>e</u> r the <u>f</u> loor

wh <u>e</u> n h <u>e</u> w <u>a</u> s p <u>a</u> intin <u>g</u>, <u>a</u> n <u>d</u>

<u>a</u> ll h <u>e</u> could <u>f</u> in <u>d</u> to us <u>e</u> wer <u>e</u> my piano <u>b</u> ooks.

NAME THAT KEY

A. Finish spelling *every other* letter (skipping letters) of the music alphabet.

Begin here ➝ **1.** F A C E G B D F A C E G

2. A C E G B D F A C E G B ← Begin here

Begin here ➝ **3.** B D F A C E G B D F A C

B. Complete the following chain of music alphabet beads by filling in each white bead with the correct letter. Each bead represents either every letter *(stepping letters)* of the music alphabet, or every other letter *(skipping letters)*. Follow the instructions on the black beads, but do not include it in your alphabet spellings.

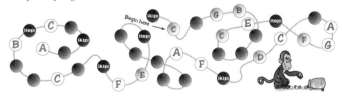

Answer on p. 160

C. Determine all the possible note names for each key shape below and write them on the appropriate key.

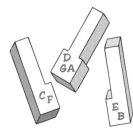

NOTES ON THE STAFF

Notes on the grand staff may be high or low.

high

low

space notes

line notes

ascending notes

descending notes

There are line notes and space notes. Line notes have a line *through* them. Space notes are placed *between* the lines.

Notes that move up the staff are **ascending** notes. Notes that move down the staff are **descending** notes.

YOUR TURN

1. Trace the brace and then trace the clef signs. Complete the clef signs that have been left unfinished. Practice by drawing four more of each clef.

2. Complete the grand staff by drawing the brace, barlines, double bar, treble clef, bass clef, and repeat sign. Then draw eight line notes moving up the grand staff and eight space notes moving down the grand staff.

Answers may vary.

3. Circle the three highest line notes and cross out the three lowest space notes.

SOMETHING'S MISSING

Add two missing parts to each grand staff below.
Bonus: Add a repeat sign to each grand staff. Add up your score below.

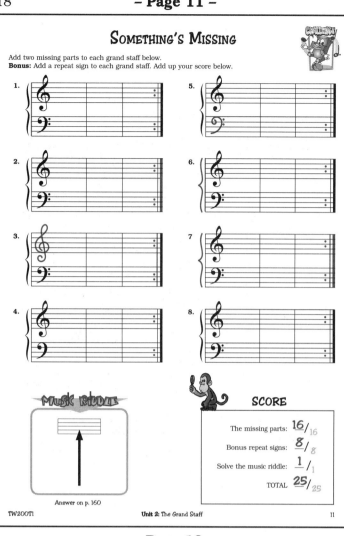

1.   5.
2.   6.
3.   7
4.   8.

MUSIC RIDDLE

Answer on p. 160

SCORE

The missing parts: **16** / 16
Bonus repeat signs: **8** / 8
Solve the music riddle: **1** / 1

TOTAL **25** / 25

GRAND STAFF PUZZLER

Fill in the blanks below with the names of the parts of the grand staff.
Carry the numbered letters over to the next page to solve the puzzler.

1. These divide the staff into measures.
   <u>B</u> <u>a</u> <u>r</u> <u>l</u> <u>i</u> <u>n</u> <u>e</u> <u>s</u>
         3

2. This is one name for the sign that wraps around the G staff line.
   <u>T</u> <u>r</u> <u>e</u> <u>b</u> <u>l</u> <u>e</u>   <u>C</u> <u>l</u> <u>e</u> <u>f</u>
     2

3. This is placed at the beginning of each grand staff.
   <u>B</u> <u>r</u> <u>a</u> <u>c</u> <u>e</u>
       4

4. This sign begins with a dot on the F staff line.
   <u>B</u> <u>a</u> <u>s</u> <u>s</u>   <u>C</u> <u>l</u> <u>e</u> <u>f</u>
    1   5

5. Barlines divide the staff into these.
   <u>M</u> <u>e</u> <u>a</u> <u>s</u> <u>u</u> <u>r</u> <u>e</u> <u>s</u>
     7

6. This is another name for the sign that begins with a dot on the F staff line.
   <u>F</u>   <u>C</u> <u>l</u> <u>e</u> <u>f</u>
      6   11

7. This sign means to play the music over again.
   <u>R</u> <u>e</u> <u>p</u> <u>e</u> <u>a</u> <u>t</u>   <u>S</u> <u>i</u> <u>g</u> <u>n</u>
       9   10

8. This is another name for the sign that wraps around the G staff line.
   <u>G</u>   <u>C</u> <u>l</u> <u>e</u> <u>f</u>
   12

9. This is placed at the end of the grand staff.
   <u>D</u> <u>o</u> <u>u</u> <u>b</u> <u>l</u> <u>e</u>   <u>B</u> <u>a</u> <u>r</u>
   8

MUSIC RIDDLE

Answer on p. 160

SOLVE THE PUZZLER

Did you know that . . .

<u>C</u> <u>r</u> <u>y</u> <u>s</u> <u>t</u> <u>a</u> <u>l</u>   <u>g</u> <u>l</u> <u>a</u> <u>s</u> <u>s</u> <u>e</u> <u>s</u>
6 4   5 2 1 3   12 3 1 5 5 7 5

<u>f</u> <u>i</u> <u>l</u> <u>l</u> <u>e</u> <u>d</u>   <u>w</u> <u>i</u> <u>t</u> <u>h</u>   <u>d</u> <u>i</u> <u>f</u> <u>f</u> <u>e</u> <u>r</u> <u>e</u> <u>n</u> <u>t</u>
11 10 3 3 7 8   10 2   8 10 11 11 7 4 7   2

<u>a</u> <u>m</u> <u>o</u> <u>u</u> <u>n</u> <u>t</u> <u>s</u>   <u>o</u> <u>f</u>   <u>w</u> <u>a</u> <u>t</u> <u>e</u> <u>r</u>   <u>c</u> <u>a</u> <u>n</u>
1   2 5   11   1 2 7 4   6 1

<u>b</u> <u>e</u>   <u>p</u> <u>l</u> <u>a</u> <u>y</u> <u>e</u> <u>d</u>   <u>b</u> <u>y</u>   <u>r</u> <u>u</u> <u>b</u> <u>b</u> <u>i</u> <u>n</u> <u>g</u>
7   9 3 1 7 8   4   10   12

<u>a</u>   <u>w</u> <u>e</u> <u>t</u>   <u>f</u> <u>i</u> <u>n</u> <u>g</u> <u>e</u> <u>r</u>   <u>g</u> <u>e</u> <u>n</u> <u>t</u> <u>l</u> <u>y</u>
1   7 2   11 10 12 7 4   12 7   2 3

<u>a</u> <u>r</u> <u>o</u> <u>u</u> <u>n</u> <u>d</u>   <u>t</u> <u>h</u> <u>e</u>   <u>r</u> <u>i</u> <u>m</u> <u>s</u> ?
1 4   8   2 7   4 10 5

<u>M</u> <u>u</u> <u>s</u> <u>i</u> <u>c</u> <u>a</u> <u>l</u>   <u>g</u> <u>l</u> <u>a</u> <u>s</u> <u>s</u> <u>e</u> <u>s</u>   <u>w</u> <u>e</u> <u>r</u> <u>e</u>   <u>a</u>
5 10 6 1 3   12 3 1 5 5 7 5   7 4 7   1

<u>p</u> <u>o</u> <u>p</u> <u>u</u> <u>l</u> <u>a</u> <u>r</u>   <u>i</u> <u>n</u> <u>s</u> <u>t</u> <u>r</u> <u>u</u> <u>m</u> <u>e</u> <u>n</u> <u>t</u>   <u>i</u> <u>n</u>
9 9 3 1 4   10 5 2 4   7 2 10

<u>V</u> <u>i</u> <u>e</u> <u>n</u> <u>n</u> <u>a</u>   <u>2</u> <u>5</u> <u>0</u>   <u>y</u> <u>e</u> <u>a</u> <u>r</u> <u>s</u>   <u>a</u> <u>g</u> <u>o</u>
10 7   1   7 1 4 5   1 12

<u>M</u> <u>o</u> <u>z</u> <u>a</u> <u>r</u> <u>t</u>   <u>w</u> <u>r</u> <u>o</u> <u>t</u> <u>e</u>   <u>t</u> <u>w</u> <u>o</u>
1 4 2   4 2 7   2

<u>p</u> <u>i</u> <u>e</u> <u>c</u> <u>e</u> <u>s</u>   <u>f</u> <u>o</u> <u>r</u>
9 10 7 6 7 5   11 4

<u>m</u> <u>u</u> <u>s</u> <u>i</u> <u>c</u> <u>a</u> <u>l</u>   <u>g</u> <u>l</u> <u>a</u> <u>s</u> <u>s</u> <u>e</u> <u>s</u> .
5 10 6 1 3   12 3 1 5 5 7 5

KEEP THE BEAT!

A. Use an X to mark the counts on which you would clap to perform these rhythms. Clap (or play) and count the rhythms. See #1 for an example. Remember to feel a steady beat before you begin.

1. $\frac{2}{4}$ (1   2)   x   x   2   x   x   2

2. $\frac{3}{4}$ (1   2   3)   X   X   3   X   X   X   2   3

3. $\frac{4}{4}$ (1   2   3   4)   X   2   3   4   X   X   3   X   X   3   4

B. Trace the rests, then draw five more of each.

quarter rest	half rest	whole rest

C. Write in the counts, then mark the counts on which you would clap to perform this rhythm. Clap and count the rhythm. Feel a steady beat before you begin. Remember to count the rests, but do not clap them.

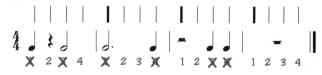

$\frac{4}{4}$ X   2   X   4   X   2   3   X   1   2   X   X   1   2   3   4

BEATS ME!

A. Add one *note* to complete each measure below, then clap and count the rhythms. Remember to feel a steady beat before you begin.

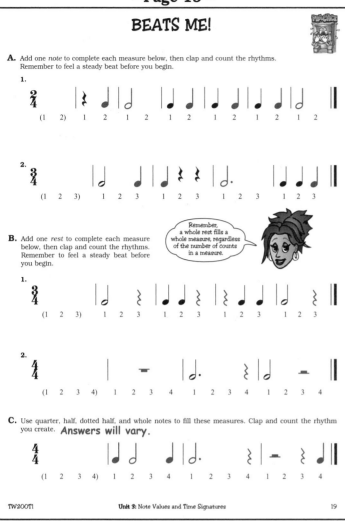

B. Add one *rest* to complete each measure below, then clap and count the rhythms. Remember to feel a steady beat before you begin.

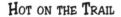

Remember, a whole rest fills a whole measure, regardless of the number of counts in a measure.

C. Use quarter, half, dotted half, and whole notes to fill these measures. Clap and count the rhythm you create. **Answers will vary.**

MOUNT BACHMORE

Make your way up the treacherous path to the famous Mt. Bachmore by stepping only on the rhythms that have been clapped correctly. Which composer do you get to visit first?

Franz Liszt ☐   Johann Sebastian Bach ☒   Ludwig van Beethoven ☐   Wolfgang Amadeus Mozart ☐

HOT ON THE TRAIL

These banana thieves have been stealing and eating bananas of various note values. Monkey has hired Johann Sebastian Holmes, the greatest music detective in the world, to help him find the thief who has eaten the most "banana" note values. Help them find out who will spend the most time in the slammer by following each slippery trail (from bottom to top) and adding up the number of counts on the peels. One count equals one year of jail time. Write each criminal's total on their mug shot sign, then circle the thief with the highest number of counts.

DARRELL   **GUS**   **TONY**

Darrell the Delinquent	**Guilty Gus**	**Talk My Way Out Tony**
34 counts/years in the slammer	**32** counts/years in the slammer	**29** counts/years in the slammer

---

NAME AND DRAW THE GUIDEPOSTS

A. Write the guidepost name beneath the shaded keys. Middle C is marked with a black dot.

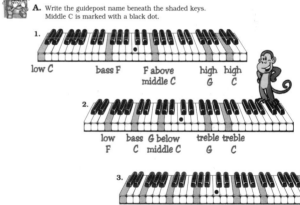

1. low C   bass F   F above middle C   high G   high C

2. low F   bass C   G below middle C   treble G   treble C

3. low C   low F   bass C   G below middle C   F above middle C   treble C   high C

B. Draw the guidepost C's on the staff below. Write the guidepost name beside each.

high C
treble C
middle C
middle C
bass C
low C

MUSIC RIDDLE

Answer on p. 160

C. Draw the guidepost G's and F's on the staff below. Write the guidepost name beside each.

high G
treble G
G below middle C
F above middle C
bass F
low F

Memorizing and being able to instantly recognize the guideposts will help you as you begin to fill in the other notes on the staff.

GUIDEPOST HIDDEN PICTURE

Shade only those notes that are guidepost **C**'s, **F**'s and **G**'s to find the hidden picture.

TW200T1   **Unit 4:** The Guideposts   25

I'M THINKING . . .

Write the name of each guidepost described below, then solve the music riddle. Complete the riddle by placing the letter names of the guideposts as indicated by the numbers in the boxes.

1. I'm thinking of a line note that is so low it requires two ledger lines below the bass or F clef staff. What is it?
   Low C

2. I'm thinking of a note that is placed in the 2nd space up from the bottom of the bass or F clef staff. What is it?
   Bass C

3. I'm thinking of a space note that hangs beneath the bottom line of the bass or F clef staff. What is it?
   Low F

4. I'm thinking of a line note that is two ledger lines above the treble or G clef staff. What is it?
   High C

5. I'm thinking of a note that is in the 2nd space down in the treble or G clef staff. What is it?
   Treble C

6. I'm thinking of a space note. It sits on top of the treble or G clef staff. What is it?
   High G

MUSIC RIDDLE
SALE 15% OFF
C C C C C C
Answer on p. 160

7. I'm thinking of a line note. The 2nd line up on the treble or G clef staff runs through it. What is it?
   Treble G

8. I'm thinking of a line note. It requires one ledger line and is placed between the two staffs of the grand staff. What is it?
   Middle C

9. I'm thinking of a space note. It requires two ledger lines above the bass or F clef staff. What is it?
   F above middle C

10. I'm thinking of a space note. It hangs beneath two ledger lines beneath the treble or G clef staff. What is it?
   G below middle C

11. I'm thinking of a line note. It requires one ledger line and is placed above the bass or F clef staff. What is it?
   Middle C

12. I'm thinking of a line note in the bass or F clef. The line that runs through it also runs between the two dots of the bass or F clef sign. What is it?
   Bass F

26   **Unit 4:** The Guideposts   TW200T1

INVERTIBLE NOTES

Drawing Stems
On notes that are lower than the middle line of the staff, draw the stem on the right side of the note, pointing up (see Low C example).

On notes that are higher than the middle line of the staff, draw the stem on the left side of the note, pointing down (see High C).

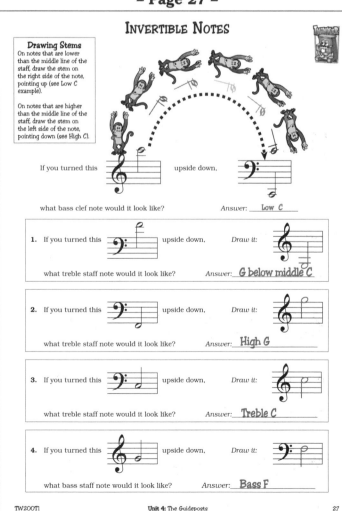

If you turned this ... upside down, what bass clef note would it look like?   Answer: **Low C**

1. If you turned this ... upside down,   Draw it:
   what treble staff note would it look like?   Answer: **G below middle C**

2. If you turned this ... upside down,   Draw it:
   what treble staff note would it look like?   Answer: **High G**

3. If you turned this ... upside down,   Draw it:
   what treble staff note would it look like?   Answer: **Treble C**

4. If you turned this ... upside down,   Draw it:
   what bass staff note would it look like?   Answer: **Bass F**

TW200T1   **Unit 4:** The Guideposts   27

SPEED READING

Practice speed-reading the keys that are shaded. Write the name beneath each key. Complete this page as fast as possible!

MUSIC RIDDLE
Answer on p. 160

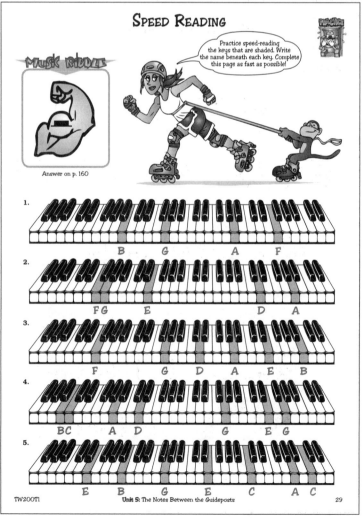

1.   B   G   A   F

2.   F G   E   D A

3.   F   G D A E B

4.   B C   A D   G   E G

5.   E   B G   G   C   A C

TW200T1   **Unit 5:** The Notes Between the Guideposts   29

Note the Possibilities

A Music Joke

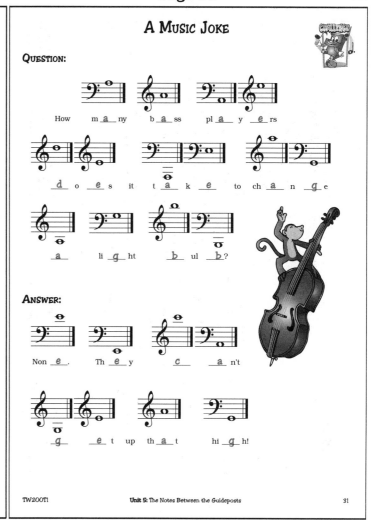

Another Music Joke . . .

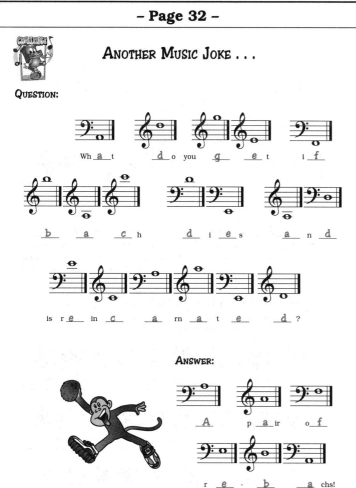

Speedy Notes

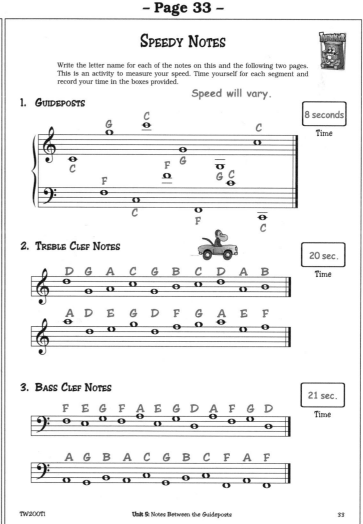

22

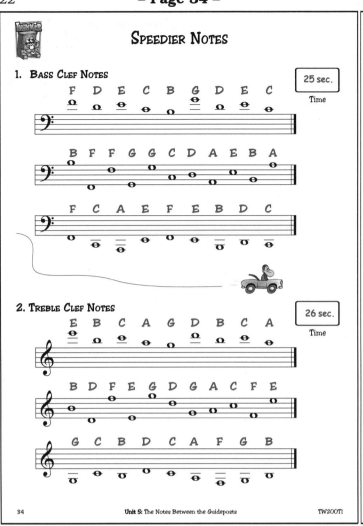

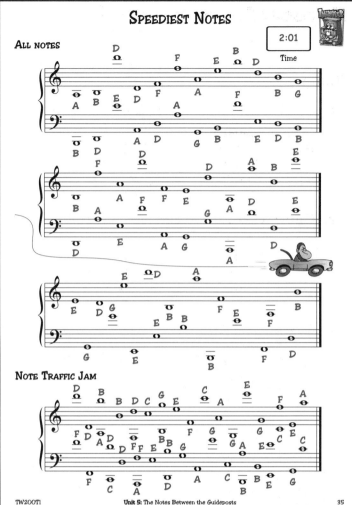

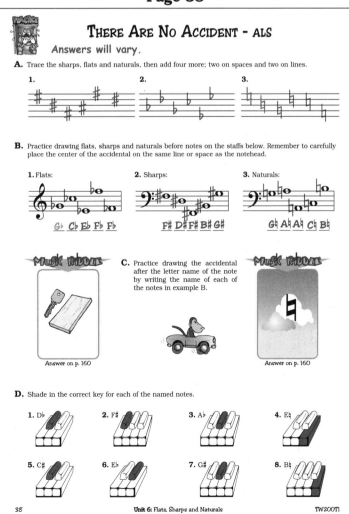

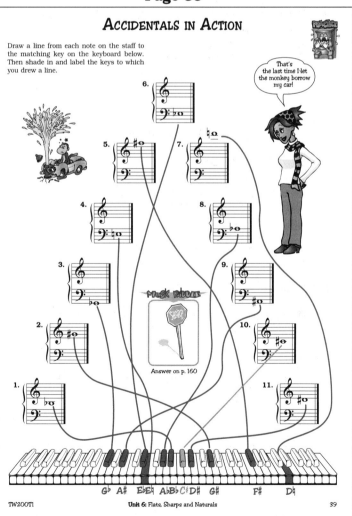

A Non-Musical Joke!

A. QUESTION

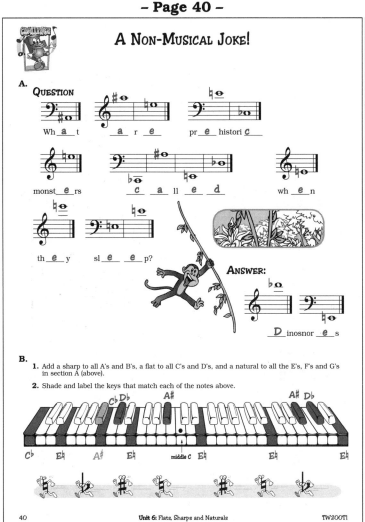

Wh _a_ t _a_ r _e_ pr _e_ histori _c_

monst _e_ rs _c_ a _l_ _l_ _e_ _d_ wh _e_ n

th _e_ y sl _e_ _e_ p?

ANSWER:

_D_ inosnor _e_ s

B.
1. Add a sharp to all A's and B's, a flat to all C's and D's, and a natural to all the E's, F's and G's in section A (above).
2. Shade and label the keys that match each of the notes above.

C♭ E♮ A♯ E♮ middle C E♮ E♮ E♮ C♭ D♭ A♯ A♯ D♭

40 Unit 6: Flats, Sharps and Naturals TW200T1

Another Non-Musical Joke!

A. QUESTION

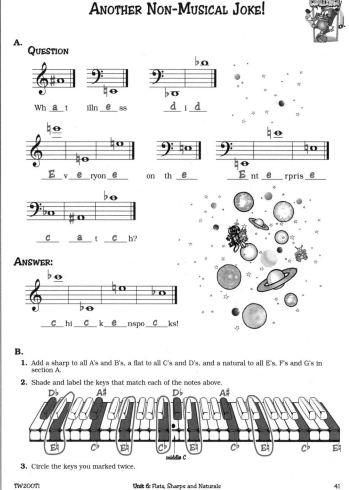

Wh _a_ t illn _e_ ss _d_ i _d_

_E_ v _e_ ryon _e_ on th _e_ _E_ nt _e_ rpris _e_

_c_ _a_ t _c_ h?

ANSWER:

_c_ hi _c_ k _e_ nspo _c_ ks!

B.
1. Add a sharp to all A's and B's, a flat to all C's and D's, and a natural to all E's, F's and G's in section A.
2. Shade and label the keys that match each of the notes above.

D♭ A♯ D♭ A♯
E♮ C♭ E♮ C♭ E♮ C♭ E♮ C♭ E♮
middle C

3. Circle the keys you marked twice.

TW200T1 Unit 6: Flats, Sharps and Naturals 41

Same, but Different

Write the enharmonic name for each note below.

1. A♭ = G♯
2. B♮ = C♭
3. C♯ = D♭
4. G♭ = F♯
5. B♯ = C♮
6. F♮ = E♯
7. B♭ = A♯
8. E♭ = D♯
9. E♮ = F♭
10. D♯ = E♭
11. F♭ = E♮
12. E♯ = F♮

Music Riddle

Answer on p. 160

42 Unit 6: Flats, Sharps and Naturals TW200T1

Learning to Walk . . . Music Style!

A. Cross out the steps and circle the skips in each staff.

B. Using only white keys, mark the keys that are a step up from the shaded notes with an X.

C. Using only white keys, mark the keys that are a skip down from the shaded notes with an X.

D. Draw a line from a letter on the left side, through an instruction, to a matching answer on the right side. Match the circles to the circles, the squares to the squares, and the triangles to the triangles. The first one has been done as an example.

Answers may vary.

Music Riddle

Answer on p. 160

A⃝	down a step	D⃝
B⃞	up a skip	A△
C△	up a step	A⃞
D⃞	down a skip	G⃞
D△	down a skip	B⃝
E⃞	up a skip	B△
F△	up a skip	E⃞
F⃞	up a step	E△
A△	down a skip	F△

TW200T1 Unit 7: Steps and Skips, Half Steps and Whole Steps 45

Half and Whole Step Challenge

A. Mark the key with an X that completes each half (H) and whole (W) step.

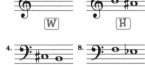

MUSIC RIDDLE

Answer on p. 160

MUSIC RIDDLE

Answer on p. 160

B. Identify the steps as half steps (H) or whole steps (W).

C. Provide the missing note for each half and whole step. *Answers may vary.*

Steps and Skips of the Caribbean

A. Begin on the lowest A on the keyboard and **skip** up. At the same time, begin on the highest A on the keyboard and **step** down. Using only the white keys, continue drawing the skips and steps with a pencil.

Mark and name the key on which you meet. __A__

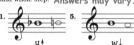

B. Begin on the lowest A on the keyboard and **step** up. At the same time, begin on the highest A on the keyboard and **skip** down. Use only the white keys.

Mark and name the key on which you meet. __A__

C.

Aye, Matey! Now that you know how to step and skip on the keyboard, try it with half and whole steps on my Caribbean Keyboard. Follow the treasure map . . . AARRRRRRRRR!

E 1. Go up 6 whole steps.
E 2. Go down 1 whole step.
D 3. Go up 8 half steps.
Bb 4. Go up 2 whole steps.
D 5. Go up 4 half steps.
F# 6. Go up 10 half steps.
E 7. Go down 9 whole steps.
Bb 8. Go up 7 half steps.
F 9. Go up 2 half steps.
G 10. Go up 13 whole steps.
On what key did you end?
A

BEGIN HERE

INTERVAL IDENTITY

A. Identify each interval as a 2nd, 3rd, 4th, 5th, 6th, 7th, 8^{ve}, or unison.

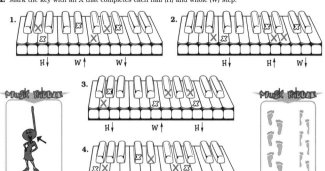

1. __4th__ 2. __5th__ 3. __7th__ 4. __6th__

5. __2nd__ 6. __5th__ 7. __4th__ 8. __8ve__ 9. __3rd__ 10. __6th__ 11. __5th__ 12. __7th__

B. Identify the intervals below as ascending (A) or descending (D).

1. __A__ 2. __A__ 3. __D__ 4. __D__

C. Identify the intervals below as melodic (M) or harmonic (H).

1. __H__ 2. __M__ 3. __M__ 4. __H__

D. Name the key up or down the indicated interval from the marked key.

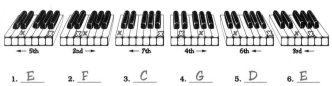

1. __E__ 2. __F__ 3. __C__ 4. __G__ 5. __D__ 6. __E__

INTERVAL UPS AND DOWNS

A. Draw the specified melodic intervals up or down from the given notes.

1.
3rd↑ 5th↑ 4th↓ 7th↑ 2nd↑ 5th↑ 4th↑

2.
3rd↓ 4th↑ 5th↑ 6th↑ 7th↑ Octave↑ 6th↓

3.
3rd↑ 2nd↑ 6th↑ 7th↑ 5th↓ 2nd↓ 6th↑

4.
4th↓ 4th↑ 7th↓ 3rd↑ Octave↑ 4th↑ 5th↑

MUSIC RIDDLE

Answer on p. 160

B. Beginning from treble C, shade in the notes in order by following the interval directions beside each note. When you are done shading you will be able to spell a word with the remaining notes.

And the word is: __beg__

– Page 52 –

THE KEYBOARD JUNGLE

Find the secret passage to the City of Gold. It lies under the final key that you mark using the directions below. Use only the white keys. Remember, when counting steps for intervals, always count the note on which you begin.

Directions:
1. ▲ 8ve   6. ▲ 6th   10. ▲ 6th
2. ▲ 4th   7. ▲ 5th   11. ▲ 4th
3. ▲ 7th   8. ▲ 8ve   12. ▼ 7th
4. ▼ 2nd   9. ▼ 7th
5. ▲ 3rd

13. ▼ 2nd   15. ▲ 4th
14. ▼ 6th   16. ▲ 7th
            17. ▲ 4th
            18. ▲ 5th

The secret passage to the City of Gold lies under: **F**

52   Unit 8: Intervals - Unisons through Octaves   TW200T1

– Page 53 –   25

CROSS STAFF INTERVALS

Sometimes intervals cross over from one staff to the next.

A. The cross-staff intervals in the first two lines have been circled. Picture each on the keyboard to help you identify the interval. Write your answers above the intervals.

B. For the third and fourth lines, see how many cross-staff intervals you can find and identify. One has been done as an example.

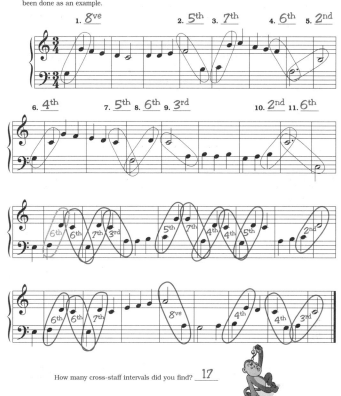

How many cross-staff intervals did you find? **17**

TW200T1   Unit 8: Intervals - Unisons through Octaves   53

– Page 54 –

UNIT 9: REVIEW #1

NOTE RACES!

Write the name beside each note as quickly as you can.

A. Guideposts

B. Bass clef notes

54   Unit 9: Review #1 - Notes   TW200T1

– Page 55 –

MORE NOTE RACES

Write the name beside each note as quickly as you can.

A. Treble clef notes

B. Grand staff notes

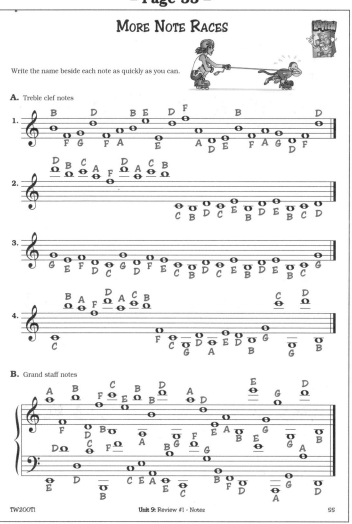

TW200T1   Unit 9: Review #1 - Notes   55

RAIN RIDDLE

One of each note (A to G) is represented on each grand staff . . . except one!
Find each missing note to solve the riddle at the bottom of the page.

RIDDLE: WHAT'S WORSE THAN RAINING CATS AND DOGS?

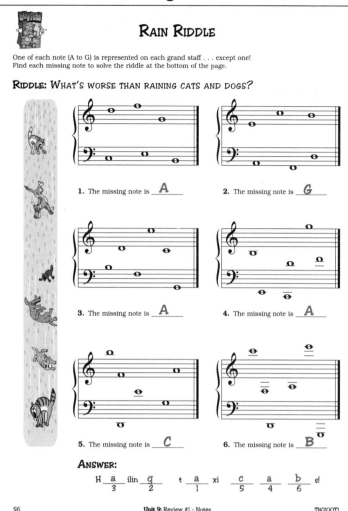

1. The missing note is **A**
2. The missing note is **G**
3. The missing note is **A**
4. The missing note is **A**
5. The missing note is **C**
6. The missing note is **B**

ANSWER:

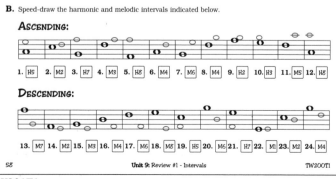

H $\frac{a}{3}$ ilin $\frac{g}{2}$ t $\frac{a}{1}$ xi $\frac{c}{5}$ $\frac{a}{4}$ $\frac{b}{6}$ s!

How MANY?

A. How many different ways can you spell the following words on the staff? You may not reuse any notes from your other versions of each word.

I have done two to help you get started.

1. BEAD   Answers will vary.
2. CAGE
3. DEAF

B. In the space below, spell as many words (3 letters or more) as you can using these letters: A B C D E F G

Answers will vary.

Use this space to spell your words: CAB, BAD, DAB, CAD, FAD, GAG, BAG, GAB, BED, FED, EBB, BEE

Draw your words with notes on this grand staff:

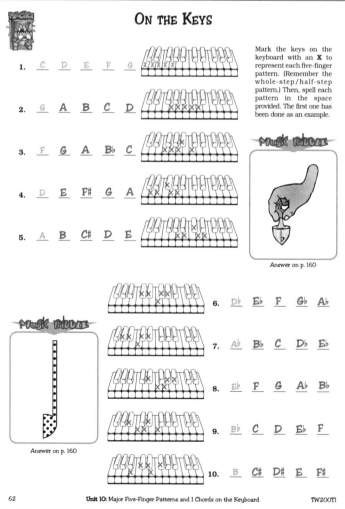

BEG   CAB   DAB   FAD   BAG   BED
BEE   BAD   CAD   GAG   GAB   FED

SPEEDY INTERVAL IDENTIFICATION

2nds, 4ths, 6ths, and octaves are **line-to-space** or **space-to-line**:

Unisons, 3rds, 5ths, and 7ths are **line-to-line** or **space-to-space**:

A. Speed-read each of the intervals below. Write the number of the interval (2, 3, 4, 5, 6, 7, 8) in the box. Write **U** for unison.

1. 2 2. 3 3. 5 4. U 5. 8 6. 5 7. U 8. 4 9. 3 10. 7 11. 2 12. 6

13. 7 14. 5 15. 4 16. 3 17. 5 18. 7 19. 4 20. 6 21. 2 22. 8 23. 6 24. 2

Answer on p. 160   Answer on p. 160

B. Speed-draw the harmonic and melodic intervals indicated below.

ASCENDING:

1. H5 2. M2 3. H7 4. M3 5. H8 6. M4 7. M6 8. M4 9. H2 10. H3 11. M5 12. H8

DESCENDING:

13. M7 14. M2 15. M3 16. M4 17. M6 18. M8 19. H5 20. M6 21. H7 22. M1 23. M2 24. M4

ON THE KEYS

1. C D E F G
2. G A B C D
3. F G A B♭ C
4. D E F♯ G A
5. A B C♯ D E

Mark the keys on the keyboard with an **X** to represent each five-finger pattern. (Remember the whole-step/half-step pattern.) Then, spell each pattern in the space provided. The first one has been done as an example.

MUSIC RIDDLE
Answer on p. 160

MUSIC RIDDLE
Answer on p. 160

6. D♭ E♭ F G♭ A♭
7. A♭ B♭ C D♭ E♭
8. E♭ F G A♭ B♭
9. B♭ C D E♭ F
10. B C♯ D♯ E F♯

VISUALIZE THE "LOOK"

A. Shade in the boxes that represent the black keys of each I chord, then write the letter names of the notes in the chord. The first exercise has been completed as an example.

Visualizing something means to picture it in your mind. It helps to visualize how each I chord looks on the keyboard.

1. E G# B
7. A C# E
2. C E G
8. F A C
3. Ab C Eb
9. Bb D F
4. B D# F#
10. F# A# C#
5. G B D
11. Db F Ab
6. D F# A
12. Eb G Bb

B. Unscramble the following five-finger patterns and I chords.

1. C F D G E → *C* D E F G
2. B C# D E A → *A B C# D E*
3. A D B C G → *G A B C D*
4. D Bb F → *Bb D F*
5. Bb G Eb → *Eb G Bb*
6. B G# E → *E G# B*
7. G Bb F A C → *F G A Bb C*
8. F# A D E G → *D E F# G A*
9. Db Eb C Bb Ab → *Ab Bb C Db Eb*
10. C# A# F# → *F# A# C#*
11. B F# D# → *B D# F#*
12. Db F Ab → *Db F Ab*

HANDY FIVE-FINGER PATTERNS

A. Write letter names on the fingers that represent the notes of the five-finger patterns.

What a "handy" way to remember five-finger patterns!

1.   2.   3.

4.   5.   6.

B. Mark the keys on the keyboard with an X to represent each I chord. Then, spell each I chord in the spaces provided. **Markings on the keyboard may vary.**

1. Db F Ab

2. F A C

3. E G# B

4. A C# E

GETTING TO THE ROOT OF THE PROBLEM

The 3rd or 5th of each I chord has been provided, but the root has not been marked. Mark each root with an **R**.

1.
2.
3.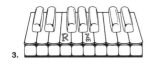
4.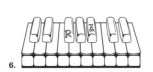
5.
6.
7.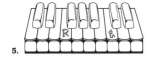
8.
9.
10.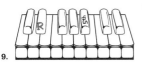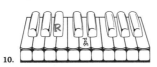

PICTURE A PATTERN

Time to practice your visualization skills.

Visualize your fingers on each note of the five-finger pattern. The spaces between your fingers represent whole and half steps.

MUSIC RIDDLE
Mr. Alarm Clock
Answer on p. 160

Think of the five-finger pattern that would be played if the marked finger were placed on the given key. Write the name of the keynote of that five-finger pattern in the box provided.

1. Ab
2. Ab
3. E
4. Eb
5. B
6. D

28

Your Turn to Draw

Follow the steps outlined below to draw major five-finger patterns on the staffs.
Use the keyboard provided to help you visualize each pattern.

Remember, visualizing the major five-finger patterns on the keyboard can be very helpful!

1. Draw five notes on the staff (remember to use steps).

2. Think of the five-finger pattern on the keyboard.

3. Start from the bottom note and add sharps or flats, as needed.

Placement on the staff may vary.

Something's Missing

A. Draw in the missing notes for each of the five-finger patterns.

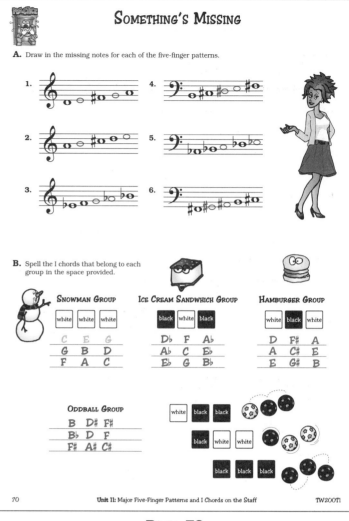

B. Spell the I chords that belong to each group in the space provided.

Snowman Group		
white	white	white
C	E	G
G	B	D
F	A	C

Ice Cream Sandwhich Group		
black	white	black
Db	F	Ab
Ab	C	Eb
Eb	G	Bb

Hamburger Group		
white	black	white
D	F#	A
A	C#	E
E	G#	B

Oddball Group		
B	D#	F#
Bb	D	F
F#	A#	C#

Making Use of the Keyboard

A. Follow the steps outlined below to draw the I chords on the staffs.
Use the keyboard provided to help you visualize each chord.

1. Beginning with the root note, draw three notes on the staff (remember to use skips).

2. Think of how the I chord looks on the keyboard.

3. Add sharps or flats according to how each chord "looks" on the keyboard.

B. The 3rd and 5th of each I chord are given. Draw the root.
Use the keyboard above to help you visualize the I chords.

Pattern Search

A. Find and circle six more hidden five-finger patterns. One has been done as an example.

Ab	Bb	D	Db	Eb	F	Gb	Ab
Ab	B	C#	D#	E	F#	E	Eb
Bb	D	E	F	G	F#	F	F
C	D	E	F	G	G#	G	G
Db	D	E	F	G	A#	A	Ab
Eb	G	A	B	C	B	B	Bb
Bb	C	D	Eb	F	C#	F	G

Chord Search

B. Find and circle six more hidden I chords. One has been done as an example.

Ab	Bb	D	F	Eb	F	G	Ab
A	B	C	D#	E	F#	E	C
B	D#	F#	F#	G#	F#	F	Eb
C	Db	Eb	F	B	G#	Gb	G
D	Db	E	F#	A#	C#	Ab	A
E#	F	A#	B	G	B	D	F#
B	Ab	D	E	F#	C	F#	G

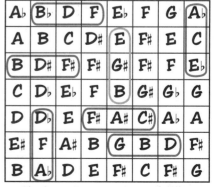

I'M THINKING OF . . .

Write the answer to each question (including sharps or flats) in the box. Use your answers (without the sharps or flats) to to help you figure out the answers to the riddles.

1. The fourth note in the B five-finger pattern is: **E**
2. The second note in the F♯ five-finger pattern is: **G♯**
3. The third note in the D♭ five-finger pattern is: **F**
4. The fifth note in the A♭ five-finger pattern is: **E♭**
5. The fourth note in the E♭ five-finger pattern is: **A♭**
6. The third note in the B♭ five-finger pattern is: **D**
7. The 3rd of the B I chord is: **D♯**
8. The 3rd of the F♯ I chord is: **A♯**
9. The root of the D♭ I chord is: **D♭**
10. The 3rd of the A♭ I chord is: **C**
11. The 5th of the E♭ I chord is: **B♭**
12. The root of the B I chord is: **B**

RIDDLE

Samuel was out for a walk when it started to rain. He did not have an umbrella and he wasn't wearing a hat. His clothes were soaked, yet not a single hair on his head got wet. How could this happen?

H e   w a s
1.   5.

b a l d
12. 8.   7.

RIDDLE

What gets wetter the more it dries?

A   t o w e l
8.   4.

Some composers that were living during these two presidential terms: Tchaikovsky, Brahms, Wagner, Verdi, Liszt, Debussy, Satie and Ravel. Scott Joplin was writing ragtime music in America.

RIDDLE

The 22nd (1885-1889) and 24th (1893-1897) presidents of the United States of America had the same parents, but were not brothers. How can this be possible?

Th e y   w e r e   the   s a m e   m a n.   G r o v e r   C l e v e l a n d
4. 1. 4.   1.   8. 4.   2. 4.   10. 1. 4. 8. 6.

s e r v e d two t e rms as pr e s i d e nt of th e Unit e d
1. 4. 6.   1.   5.   4.   1.   3. 1.   4. 6.

St a t e s, but   th e   t e rms   w e r e   not   c o ns e c utive.
5. 4.   11.   1.   1. 4.   1. 4.   10. 1. 10. 4.

COUNT OFF!

As a shortcut, use the plus sign "+" for the word "and" when writing the counts of a rhythm.

A. Write in the counts, then clap and count the rhythms. Clap once for each note. Remember to feel a steady beat before you begin. If a rhythm includes eighth notes, use the word "and" when counting.

1. $\frac{2}{4}$
say: (1+2+) 1+2+ 1+2+ 1 + 2 + 1+2+ 1+2+   1+2+ 1 + 2 + 1+2+

2. $\frac{3}{4}$
say: (1+2+3+) 1+2+ 3+ 1+2+3 + 1+2+ 3+   1+2+3 + 1 + 2 + 3 + 1+2+3+

3. $\frac{4}{4}$
say: (1+2+3+4+) 1+2+3+4+ 1 + 2 + 3+4+ 1+2+3+4+ 1 + 2 + 3 + 4 +

B. Using only eighth notes (♫ or ♪) and eighth rests (⁷), fill in the missing beats for each of the rhythms below. Write in the counts, then clap and count the rhythms. Remember to use "and" (+) when counting eighth notes. **Answers will vary.**

1. $\frac{2}{4}$
say: (1+2+) 1+2+ 1+2+ 1 + 2 + 1 + 2 + 1+2+ 1 + 2 + 1 + 2 + 1+2+

2. $\frac{3}{4}$
say: (1+2+3+) 1+2+3+ 1+2+3 + 1 + 2 + 3 1+2+3 + 1+2+3 + 1+2+3 +

3. $\frac{4}{4}$
say: (1+2+3+4+) 1+2+3+4+ 1 + 2 + 3 + 4 + 1+2+3+4+ 1 + 2 + 3 + 4 +

EIGHTH NOTE MATH

Circle the equations below that are correct. Fix any incorrect equation by adding or crossing out eighth notes.

1. ♩ = ♫ *(circled)*
2. ♩ = ♫♫✗
3. ♩. = ♫♫♩
4. ○ = ♫♫♫♫ *(circled)*
5. ♩ = ♩ *(circled)*
6. ○ = ♩ ♩ ♩ *(circled)*
7. ♩. = ♩ ♩ ♩
8. ○ = ♩ ♫ ♫

The words "note value" refer to the number of counts for a given note. The note value of a quarter note is one count.

TRUE (T) OR FALSE (F)

1. **T** There are three quarter notes in a dotted half note.
2. **T** There are two eighth notes in a quarter note.
3. **T** There are four eighth notes in a half note.
4. **F** There are seven eighth notes in a whole note.
5. **T** There are six eighth notes in a dotted half note.
6. **T** There are two half notes in a whole note.

YOU CREATE THE RHYTHM

Add notes to complete the measures below. Use at least one of each of these note value in each exercise: whole notes, dotted half notes, half notes, quarter notes, and eighth notes. After writing the counts, clap and count your rhythms. **Answers will vary.**

1. $\frac{4}{4}$
(Feel the beat) 1+2+ 3 + 4 + 1+2+3 + 4 + 1 + 2 + 3 + 4 + 1+2+3+4+

2. $\frac{3}{4}$
(Feel the beat) 1 + 2 + 3 +   1 + 2 + 3 + 1 + 2 + 3 + 1 + 2 + 3 +

SUBDIVIDING IS WHERE IT'S AT!

example: $\frac{3}{4}$

Lines to show the eighth beats: | | | | | | | | | | | | | | | | | |

The eighth notes in each beat: ♪♪♪♪♪♪   ♪♪♪♪♪♪   ♪♪♪♪♪♪

Count: 1 + 2 + 3 +   1 + 2 + 3 +   1 + 2 + 3 +

Clap: *   *   * * *

Draw lines to indicate the number of eighth notes contained in each note or rest for the rhythms below. Subdivide (feel the eighth notes in each note or rest) as you clap and count each rhythm.

SUBDIVIDING is feeling the smaller note values in each beat of a rhythm. When counting a rhythm, subdivide by the smallest note value.

1. $\frac{4}{4}$

2. $\frac{2}{4}$

3. $\frac{3}{4}$

EIGHTH NOTE BREAK DOWN

How many eighth beats are in each circle? Write your answers in the circles beneath each rhythm. (**Hint:** Calculate the whole rest in $\frac{4}{4}$ time.)

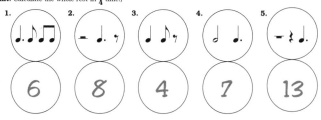

1. **6**
2. **8**
3. **4**
4. **7**
5. **13**

ADD IT UP!

Add up the counts in each box and write the total number in the space provided. ♩ = 1 beat
Shade in the box that contains the most beats.

Example:
| ♩ ♩ ♩ or o o o |
| 6 counts / 12 counts |

3.
| ♫♫ or ♩ ♩ ♩ |
4 counts / 5 counts

6.
| o ♫ or ♩ ♩ |
6 counts / 5 counts

1.
| ♩ ♩ or ♩ ♩ ♩ |
4 counts / 5 counts

4.
| ♩ o o or ♩ ♩. |
9 counts / 5 counts

7.
| o ♩. o ♩. or ♩ o o ♩ |
14 counts / 12 counts

2.
| ♩. ♩. or ♩ ♩ ♩ ♩ |
5 counts / 4 counts

5.
| ♩. ♩. ♩. or ♩ ♩ ♩ ♩ |
7 counts / 8 counts

8.
| o ♩ ♫ or ♩ ♩ ♩ |
8 counts / 6 counts

HOW'S YOUR MUSIC MATH?

Solve the Music Math equations below. ♩ = 1 beat
(**Hint:** Calculate the whole rest in 4/4 time.)

1. ♩ + ♩. + 𝄽 + ♩ = **7** counts OR **14** eighth notes

2. ♩. + ♩ + 𝄾 + ♪ = **3** counts OR **6** eighth notes

3. ♫ + o + ▬ + o = **11** counts OR **22** eighth notes

4. ♩. + 𝄾 + ▬ + 𝄾 = **6½** counts OR **13** eighth notes

5. o + ▬ + ♩. + ▬ = **11** counts OR **22** eighth notes

6. ♫ + ♩. + ♪ + ♩. = **4½** counts OR **9** eighth notes

7. 𝄽 + o + ♩. + o = **12** counts OR **24** eighth notes

8. ▬ + ♩. + 𝄾 + ♩. = **7½** counts OR **15** eighth notes

LET'S SPEND SOME MONEY!

Draw one note or rest on each coin to equal the cost of each item in eighth notes. Use each note and rest pictured below at least once. Use at least one dotted quarter note in each set of coins. (**Hint:** Calculate the whole rest in 4/4 time.)

EXAMPLE: ♪ ♫ ♩ ♩. ♩ ♩. 𝄾 𝄽 ▬ —

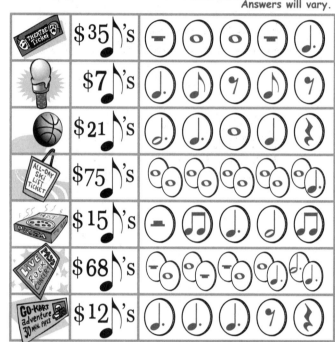

Answers will vary.

Find the path to the top of the tree. Begin on a rope ladder at the bottom and climb through a time signature. Next choose a rope ladder that has the correct number of notes and rests to make up one measure in that time signature. (If the first time signature you climb through doesn't work, try a different one.) Continue until you reach the top.

UNIT 13: REVIEW #2
THE VALUE OF NOTES AND RESTS

A. Assign a time signature to each one-measure rhythm.

1. 3/4 ♩. ♪ ♩
2. 4/4 𝄽 ♩ ♩
3. 2/4 ♩ ♩
4. 2/4 ♩. ♪
5. 4/4 ♩. 𝄽
6. 2/4 𝄾 ♩ ♩
7. 4/4 ♩. ♪ ♩
8. 3/4 ♩ 𝄾 ♩
9. 2/4 ♩ 𝄾 ♩
10. 4/4 ♫ —
11. 3/4 𝄾 ♪ ♩ ♩
12. 3/4 𝄽 𝄽 ♩

B. From the rhythms above, choose and copy four one-measure rhythms for each of the time signature below in any order you choose. Write in the counts below each. Clap and count your rhythms.

Answers may vary.

1. 2/4 ♩ | ♫ | 𝄾 ♪ ♪ | ♩. | ♪ ♩ | ♩ | 𝄾 ♪ ♩ ‖

2. 3/4 ♩. | ♪ ♪ ♩ | ♪ ♫ 𝄾 ♪ | 𝄽 ♪ ♩ ♪ | 𝄽 𝄽 ♫ | ‖

3. 4/4 𝄽 ♩ ♩ | ♩. 𝄽 | ♩. ♩ ♪ | ♫ ♩ — ‖

C. Draw the following notes and rests in order from the smallest value to the greatest value in the box provided. (Note: Some notes and rests will have the same value.)

Answers may vary.

♩. ♪ ♩ — 𝄽 ♫ ♩. o 𝄾

| ♪ 𝄾 𝄽 ♫ ♩ ♩. ▬ ♩. o |

> "Value" means how many beats are in each note or rest.

DRIPPING RHYTHM TREE

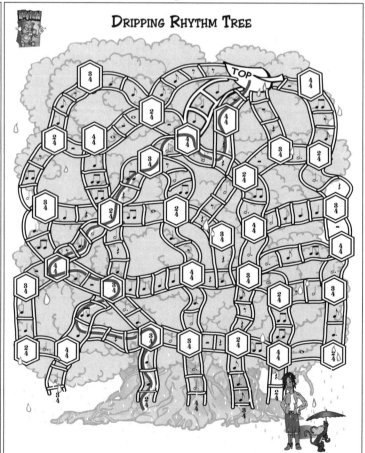

Search High and Low

Circle enough note values to fill one measure of the designated time signature. Find ten rhythms for each time signature that do not overlap each other.

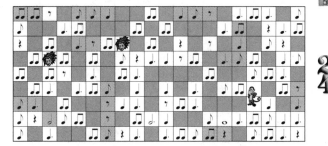

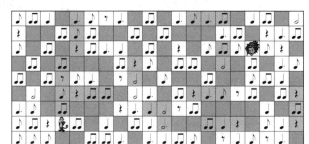

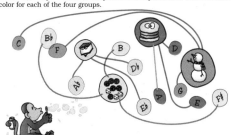

Give Me Five!

A. The whole (w) and half (h) step pattern of all major five-finger patterns is:

♩ W ♩ W ♩ H ♩ W ♩

B. Fill in the correct letters and add sharps or flats for the following major five-finger patterns. Add sharps and flats to some of the given notes as necessary to correctly spell the five-finger pattern.

1. _C_ D _E_ F G   4. Eb F G _Ab_ _Bb_   7. Ab _Bb_ C _Db_ _Eb_

2. F G A _Bb_ _C_   5. Gb _Ab_ _Bb_ Cb Db   8. _G_ A _B_ C D

3. _A_ B _C#_ D E   6. D E F# _G_ _A_   9. F# G# A# _B_ _C#_

C. Four of these major five-finger patterns are marked incorrectly. Circle and fix the mistakes.

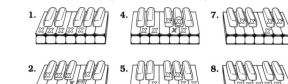

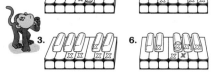

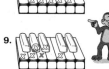

D. Visualize the major five-finger patterns described below and name them in the boxes provided.

1. This five-finger pattern has 4 sharps: F#

2. This five-finger pattern has 3 sharps: B

3. This five-finger pattern has 1 flat: F

4. This five-finger pattern has 2 flats: Bb

5. This five-finger pattern has 3 flats: Eb

6. This five-finger pattern has 2 sharps: E

7. These two five-finger patterns have no sharps or flats: C G

8. These two five-finger patterns have 4 flats: Db Ab

Number 1 in a Major Way

A. Is the arrow pointing to the Root, 3rd, or 5th of each triad?

1. 5th   2. 3rd   3. R   4. 3rd

B. Match each major I chord to the picture that represents it. Use a different color for each of the four groups.

Remember these groupings are based on how each major I chord looks on the keyboard.

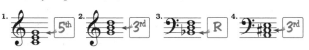

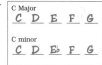

C. Complete each I chord.

1. _D_ F# A   4. _C_ E G   7. _Eb_ G _Bb_

2. _E_ G# _B_   5. B D# _F#_   8. _F#_ A# _C#_

3. _Db_ F _Ab_   6. _Ab_ _C_ Eb   9. _Bb_ _D_ F

D. Add accidentals to the following major I chords.

1. D   2. B   3. Ab   4. F#

Major and Minor Practice

First shade the five keys that represent the major and minor five-finger patterns. Next, spell the five-finger patterns.

Markings on the keyboard may vary by octave.

1.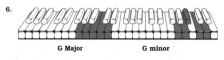
   C Major — C minor

   C Major: _C_ _D_ _E_ _F_ _G_
   C minor: _C_ _D_ _Eb_ _F_ _G_

2.
   C# Major — C# minor

   C# Major: _C#_ _D#_ _E#_ _F#_ _G#_
   C# minor: _C#_ _D#_ _E_ _F#_ _G#_

3.
   F# Major — F# minor

   F# Major: _F#_ _G#_ _A#_ _B_ _C#_
   F# minor: _F#_ _G#_ _A_ _B_ _C#_

4.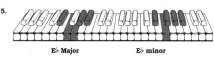
   A Major — A minor

   A Major: _A_ _B_ _C#_ _D_ _E_
   A minor: _A_ _B_ _C_ _D_ _E_

5.
   Eb Major — Eb minor

   Eb Major: _Eb_ _F_ _G_ _Ab_ _Bb_
   Eb minor: _Eb_ _F_ _Gb_ _Ab_ _Bb_

6.
   G Major — G minor

   G Major: _G_ _A_ _B_ _C_ _D_
   G minor: _G_ _A_ _Bb_ _C_ _D_

MAJOR FIVE-FINGER PATTERN SUDOKU

A. Complete the grid so that each row, column and 3x2 box contains every digit from 1 to 6.

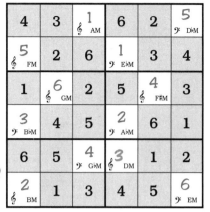

4	3	1 🎼 AM	6	2	5 𝄢 D♭M
5 🎼 FM	2	6	1 𝄢 E♭M	3	4
1	6 🎼 GM	2	5	4 🎼 F#M	3
3 𝄢 B♭M	4	5	2 𝄢 A♭M	6	1
6	5	4 𝄢 G♭M	3 🎼 DM	1	2
2 🎼 BM	1	3	4	5	6 𝄢 EM

B. Draw the five-finger pattern named in the white boxes in the puzzle above on the matching staff below. Treble clef #3 in D Major has been completed as an example.

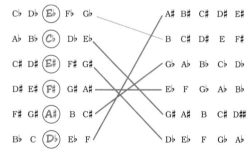

1. AM
2. BM
3. DM
4. F#M
5. FM
6. GM

1. E♭M
2. A♭M
3. B♭M
4. G♭M
5. D♭M
6. EM

MAJOR AND MINOR FIVE-FINGER PATTERN CHAINS

Finish spelling the five-finger patterns in each chain by transferring the last two or three letters to the next line as directed. See the beginning example.

A.

MAJOR	A	B	C#	D	E
MINOR	D	E	F	G	A
MINOR	G	A	B♭	C	D
MAJOR	B♭	C	D	E♭	F
MAJOR	E♭	F	G	A♭	B♭
MINOR	A♭	B♭	C♭	D♭	E♭
MAJOR	C♭	D♭	E♭	F♭	G♭

MUSIC RIDDLE

Answer on p. 160

MUSIC RIDDLE

Answer on p. 160

B.

MAJOR	E	F#	G#	A	B
MINOR	A	B	C	D	E
MAJOR	C	D	E	F	G
MINOR	F	G	A♭	B♭	C
MAJOR	A♭	B♭	C	D♭	E♭
MAJOR	D♭	E♭	F	G♭	A♭

REAL LIFE ENHARMONICS

A. Each major or minor five-finger pattern on the right has a matching enharmonic spelling on the left. Draw a line to connect each match. Then fill in the missing letters.

C♭ D♭ (E♭) F♭ G♭   A# B# C# D# E#

A♭ B♭ (C♭) D♭ E♭   B C# D# E F#

C# D# (E#) F# G#   G♭ A♭ B♭ C♭ D♭

D# E# (F#) G# A#   E♭ F G♭ A♭ B♭

F# G# (A#) B C#   G# A# B C# D##

B♭ C (D♭) E♭ F   D♭ E♭ F G♭ A♭

B. Decide whether the enharmonic patterns you matched above are Major or minor and list them here. One has already been completed.

MAJOR Enharmonic Five-Finger Patterns

B	=	C♭
G♭	=	F#
D♭	=	C#

MINOR Enharmonic Five-Finger Patterns

A#	=	B♭
E♭	=	D#
G#	=	A♭

C. Write some "real life" enharmonics below.

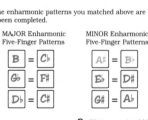

Although "enharmonic" is a music term, it is fun to think of real-life enharmonics. For example, a lollipop can also be called a sucker.

REAL-LIFE ENHARMONICS
Answers will vary.
1. Lollipop = Sucker
2. Boat = Ship
3. Soda = Pop
4. Rug = Carpet

FIVE-FINGER PATTERN GRAFFITI

Someone has drawn five-finger pattern graffiti on this building's wall. Circle and fix the mistakes in the major and minor five-finger patterns.

E♭ MAJOR = E♭ F (G♭) (A) B♭

F# MINOR = F# G# (A#) B C#

A MINOR = A B (C#) D E

C# MAJOR = C# (D# E# F# A#)

F# MINOR = F# G# A B C#

C# MAJOR = C# (D E F#) A#

E♭ MAJOR = E♭ A♭ B♭ C D♭

D♭ MAJOR = D♭ (E♭) F G♭ (A♭)

A MINOR = A B C D E

E♭ MAJOR = E♭ F (G# A) B♭

A MAJOR = A B C# D E

D MAJOR = D (C) F G A

B MINOR = B C# D E F#

D MAJOR = D C# (E) F#

B♭ MINOR = B♭ C D E♭ F

G MINOR = G A B♭ C D

E MAJOR = E F# A# B (C)

A MAJOR = A B C# (D) E

Five-Finger Pattern Search

Use a highlighter to mark the notes that make up each five-finger pattern in *Five Finger Waltz*. Label each.
Hint: Cross off the pattern names as you go. Some patterns are ascending and others are descending.

FIVE FINGER WALTZ

Zundel Shelzi

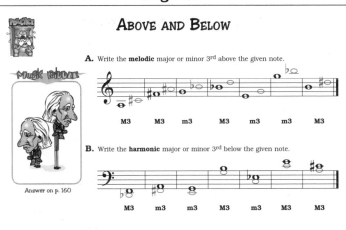

TW200T1   Unit 14: Minor Five-Finger Patterns and i Chords   93

Mark It and Circle It

A. Mark a key on each keyboard to represent the Major or minor 3rd according to the heading.

| Up a Major 3rd | Down a Major 3rd | Up a minor 3rd | Down a minor 3rd |

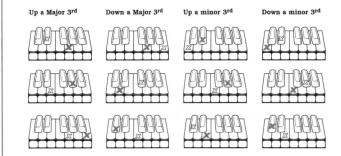
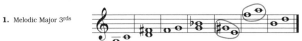

B. Circle all the matching answers for each.

1. Melodic Major 3rds
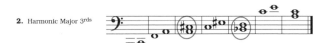

2. Harmonic Major 3rds

3. Melodic minor 3rds

4. Harmonic minor 3rds

TW200T1   Unit 15: Major and Minor Thirds and Triads   97

Above and Below

A. Write the **melodic** major or minor 3rd above the given note.

M3   M3   m3   M3   m3   m3   M3

B. Write the **harmonic** major or minor 3rd below the given note.

M3   m3   m3   M3   m3   M3   M3

Answer on p. 160

C. Follow the Keyboard Travel Itinerary to discover your final destination. Begin on the key marked with the X. Write your answer in the box provided below.

Keyboard Travel Itinerary
1. Up a Major 3rd
2. Down a minor 3rd
3. Down two minor 3rds
4. Down a Major 3rd
5. Up a minor 3rd
6. Down five Major 3rds
7. Down a minor 3rd
8. Down a Major 3rd
9. Up seven minor 3rds
10. Up a Major 3rd

Final Destination:
A

98   Unit 15: Major and Minor Thirds and Triads   TW200T1

String Me Along

Solve the puzzle below by stringing the letter beads directly across from each other together with two beads from the center to make a true statement. One has been done as an example. How many beads can you string?

Answers may vary.

TW200T1   Unit 15: Major and Minor Thirds and Triads   99

LABEL WITH CARE

A. Name the root, third, or fifth of each triad.

1. 5th: **Bb**   2. root: **C#**   3. 3rd: **F#**   4. 5th: **C#**   5. 3rd: **D**

B. Label each triad with its name and quality.

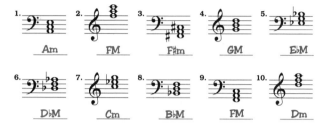

1. **Am**   2. **FM**   3. **F#m**   4. **GM**   5. **EbM**

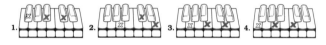

6. **DbM**   7. **Cm**   8. **BbM**   9. **FM**   10. **Dm**

C. Mark the keys that complete each **major triad**. The root is marked with an X.

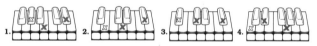

1.   2.   3.   4.

D. Mark the keys that complete each **minor triad**. The root is marked with an X.

1.   2.   3.   4.

Unit 15: Major and Minor Thirds and Triads

GONE MISSING

This is how accidentals are drawn next to chords.

The missing notes may be the root, the third, or the fifth.

Speaking of missing, I think I'm also missing some notes!

A. Complete each triad by adding the missing notes and accidentals.

1. **Am**   2. **DM**   3. **Fm**

4. **DbM**   5. **AbM**   6. **BM**

7. **GbM**   8. **Gm**   9. **FM**

B. Draw the following triads. Remember the accidentals.

1. **Bm**   2. **Dm**   3. **AM**   4. **EM**

5. **Abm**   6. **Bbm**   7. **Em**   8. **D#m**

Unit 15: Major and Minor Thirds and Triads

MAJOR MUNCHIES TRIAD KEYPAD

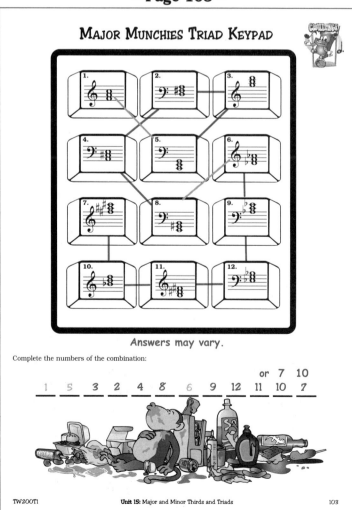

Answers may vary.

Complete the numbers of the combination:

1 5 3 2 4 8 6 9 12 11 10 7   or 7 10

Unit 15: Major and Minor Thirds and Triads

THE ADVENTURES OF JOHANN SEBASTIAN HOLMES

Johann Sebastian Holmes is the greatest music detective in the world! Be his apprentice as he solves the following music cases. He has been given many music examples that have hidden triads in them. His method for solving these mysteries involves looking at all the notes and arranging them line-line-line or space-space-space so they form root position triads. Write the triad on the staff. Then, write the name of the triad and it's quality beneath the staff. Observe Johann Sebastian Holmes as he cracks one of his cases, then you try the others.

Ah ha! I see 2 C's, 2 E's and 4 G's. Hmmm ...C, E, G. Why yes, of course! What we are seeing here is a classic example of a C Major triad.

Case #1 **CM**

Case #2 **Gm**   Case #3 **EbM**

Case #4 **CM**   Case #5 **Dm**

Unit 15: Major And Minor Thirds and Triads

WORLD'S GREATEST MUSIC DETECTIVE

Case #6 B♭m

Case #7 Bm

Case #8 FM

Case #9 Em

Case #10 Dm

Case #11 AM

Case #12 D♭M

SCRAMBLED TERMS

The monkey has been at it again, and now some of the terms that you have learned have been scrambled below. Unscramble them and spell them correctly in the boxes provided. Connect each term to its definition. If the term has a sign, draw a line from the term, through the sign, to the definition. Use a different color for each term.

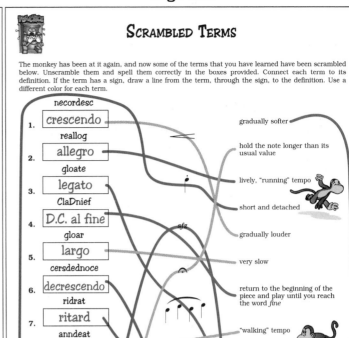

1. necordesc — **crescendo**
2. reallog — **allegro**
3. gloate — **legato**
4. ClaDnief — **D.C. al fine**
5. gloar — **largo**
6. cersdednoce — **decrescendo**
7. ridrat — **ritard**
8. anndeat — **andante**
9. sranzoofd — **sforzando**
10. centac — **accent**
11. cactoast — **staccato**
12. arfmeat — **fermata**

Definitions:
- gradually softer
- hold the note longer than its usual value
- lively, "running" tempo
- short and detached
- gradually louder
- very slow
- return to the beginning of the piece and play until you reach the word *fine*
- "walking" tempo
- emphasized
- smooth and connected
- with force — a sudden, strong accent
- gradually slowing

THINGS COULD BE WORSE!

Fill in the blanks of this story with a music term that makes the most sense to you. There are many possibilities. Be prepared to defend your answers. You may use a term more than once.

crescendo	andante	accent	mezzo piano
decrescendo	D.C. al fine	sforzando	mezzo forte
accelerando	allegro	legato	staccato
tempo	slur	fermata	forte
dynamics	tie	flat	largo
sharp	piano	natural	ritardando

It was Tuesday and Charlie didn't want to go to school because today was the term test for math. He reluctantly threw his books into his backpack **1.** accent/largo and headed out the door feeling **2.** flat as he peddled his bike **3.** largo to school.

Math was the first class of the day. Charlie hunkered down in his seat and began studying **4.** allegro for the test. The bell rang **5.** sforzando/forte and the teacher entered the classroom **6.** allegro, her shoes making a **7.** staccato/accent sound. Charlie felt his heartbeat **8.** accelerando as the teacher began handing out the tests. Out of the corner of his eye he saw Laura enter **9.** andante and confidently take her seat. She was looking very **10.** sharp/natural. Charlie thought to himself, "I wonder what she would say if I ever asked her out?" At that moment, the teacher dropped a copy of the test **11.** allegro on his desk and all other thoughts went out of his brain. The test seem to last **12.** fermata.

Finally it was over and Charlie **13.** sforzando realized that he was starving! He headed **14.** allegro to the cafeteria. When he arrived he remembered that he was **15.** flat broke. He spied his buddy, Paul, across the room. With a sigh of relief he headed over **16.** allegro/legato to borrow some money. On the way he saw Laura again. She was sitting by herself and he thought that if he hurried **17.** accelerando he might be able to sit with her before she was surrounded by her **18.** forte friends.

Paul, whom Charlie thought of in super hero terms as 'captain really great guy,' came through and soon Charlie was heading towards Laura's table as **19.** allegro as he could. He was so focused on his goal that he didn't watch where he was going and tripped **20.** sforzando over someone's foot! Everything seemed to go into **21.** largo motion as his plate crashed **22.** accent/sforzando to the floor. Applesauce flew off the plate right onto Laura's face. Carrot sticks bounced on the floor with a **23.** staccato/accent sound. The honey-slathered roll stuck to the ceiling with a splat. His drink carton busted open and sent **24.** slurred/legato sprays of orange mystery drink all over the teacher on lunchroom duty. The entire lunchroom went completely **25.** piano for a **26.** fermata period. Then the students broke into riotous laughter rising with a **27.** crescendo to **28.** forte. Charlie wished he could **29.** D.C. al fine the whole situation.

With **30.** slurred/legato motions, Charlie reached up to pull the roll stuck on the ceiling down to its **31.** natural/flat position. The honey made his fingers sticky like they were **32.** tied together. How could he ever face Laura again after making such a **33.** forte fool of himself. He couldn't believe what happened next. Laura bent down at a deliberate **34.** tempo, wiped the applesauce from her face and began to **35.** allegro/andante pick up the mess. She wasn't laughing at him. She was helping him! Charlie felt great! Maybe there *was* hope!

At that moment the principal walked in. The students' **36.** dynamics became very **37.** piano with a **38.** decrescendo. It was over, the food was cleaned up, and the students turned their attention back to their meals. Laura said, "You must still be hungry. Why don't you **39.** D.C. al fine the lunch line and get another plate? Then you can join me and we'll eat lunch **40.** mezzo piano together. Charlie felt like he was ten feet tall! One hundred math tests couldn't ruin his day now!

HIGH MARKS FOR MOZART

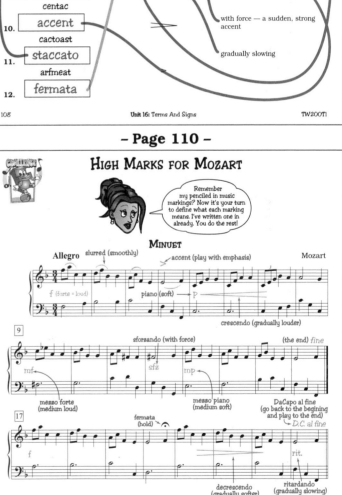

Remember my penciled in music markings? Now it's your turn to define what each marking means. I've written one in already. You do the rest!

MINUET   Mozart

Allegro — slurred (smoothly) — accent (play with emphasis)

f (forte = loud) — piano (soft) p — crescendo (gradually louder)

sforzando (with force) sfz — mf — mp — (the end) fine

mezzo forte (medium loud) — mezzo piano (medium soft) — DaCapo al fine (go back to the begining and play to the end) D.C. al fine

fermata (hold) — f — decrescendo (gradually softer) — ritardando (gradually slowing) rit.

MUSIC RIDDLE

MATA

Answer on p. 160

Aaaahh. Time for a candy break while my students write in the definitions.

Venting with Terms!

Match each term or symbol to an "annoying" description on the right side of the page.
One has been done as an example. Answers will vary.

Box	Term/Symbol
2	*p*
14	*mp*
11	*mf*
9	*f*
17	<
21	>
7	>
20	largo
18	andante
8	allegro
12	*sfz*
1	*rit.*
19	♯
16	♭
22	♮
13	*legato*
3	♪
15	♫
5	♫
10	𝆕
4	*D.C. al fine*
6	*fine*

1. The driver in front of you is riding his brakes.
2. The hissing of a snake.
3. The yapping of a little dog.
4. Having to put things away every time I'm done with them . . . sometimes I'm going to use them again!
5. People who almost stop before they turn a corner in their car.
6. The final bell that signals lunch break is over—I could stay at lunch all day!
7. Someone banging with a hammer.
8. A speeding car on the freeway that cuts everybody off.

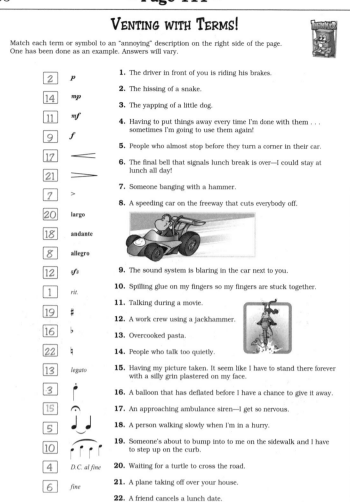

9. The sound system is blaring in the car next to you.
10. Spilling glue on my fingers so my fingers are stuck together.
11. Talking during a movie.
12. A work crew using a jackhammer.
13. Overcooked pasta.
14. People who talk too quietly.
15. Having my picture taken. It seem like I have to stand there forever with a silly grin plastered on my face.
16. A balloon that has deflated before I have a chance to give it away.
17. An approaching ambulance siren—I get so nervous.
18. A person walking slowly when I'm in a hurry.
19. Someone's about to bump into to me on the sidewalk and I have to step up on the curb.
20. Waiting for a turtle to cross the road.
21. A plane taking off over your house.
22. A friend cancels a lunch date.

It's All About the Rhythm

Add rhythms to this nursery rhyme using the steps described on page 112.
Choose a time signature and write it in the box at the beginning of each poem.
The first example has been started for you. Answers will vary.

Rythms may vary.

A. My Son, John

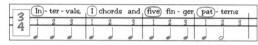

B. Teach Her Some More

Pick Me Up and Get Me Going!

All of these examples have a pickup note(s) or upbeat(s). Add rhythms using the steps described on pages 112 and 113. Choose a time signature and write it in the box at the beginning of each example. Answers will vary.

Answers may vary.

Example:

Remember, these examples begin with an incomplete measure, so they will end with an incomplete measure.

1.
2.
3.
4.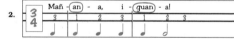
5.
6.

Give Me Three

Notate three different rhythms in three different meters for the poem below. Then decide which version you like the best and put its corresponding letter in the box provided below. Answers will vary.

Answers may vary.

A.

Three beautiful women, witty and wise,
Had crooked smiles and lovely eyes.
They practiced forever, the piano to play,
This made them mean and cranky all day!

B.

Three beautiful women, witty and wise,
Had crooked smiles and lovely eyes.
They practiced forever, the piano to play,
This made them mean and cranky all day!

C.

Three beautiful women, witty and wise,
Had crooked smiles and lovely eyes.
They practiced forever, the piano to play,
This made them mean and cranky all day!

Your Favorite Version

REPETITION AND SEQUENCE

A. Label each example with "R" for repetition or "S" for sequence in the box beside it.

 1.   R

 2.   S

 3.   S

4.  Me!   Me again!   Me again!   S

 5.   S

B. Write your own music examples according to the label.   *Answers will vary.*

 1.   repetition

 2.   sequence

 3.   sequence

 4.   repetition

 5.   sequence

LOOK AROUND YOU

There are examples of repetition and sequence all around us. In the city street below, circle examples of repetition in blue. Circle examples of sequences in orange. Many different answers are possible. Discuss this page with your teacher.

Answers may vary.

"COMPOSE" A POEM

A. Finish writing the following poem:

Fast	cars	are	red
Summer	grass	is	green
I	love	to	eat
Rocky	Road	ice	cream!

OR . . . write your own four-line poem.

B. Add a time signature and rhythm to your poem. Follow the steps as described in **Unit 17.**

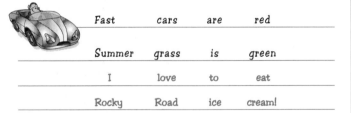

2/4 Fast cars are red
Summer grass is green
I love to eat
Rocky Road ice cream!

POETIC COMPOSITION

Using the ideas for composing a melody in this unit, add pitches to the rhythm you composed on the Challenge page.

The composer is the person who writes the music. The lyricist is the person who writes the lyrics (words) for the music.

Summer Fun
Title

Zundel Shelzi   **Zundel Shelzi**
Lyricist   Composer

Fast cars are red   summer grass is green

I love to eat   rocky road   Ice cream!

Remember to include things like the clef sign, the time signature, tempo, barlines, and any music markings (terms, articulation, dynamics) to help the performer know how you would like your music played.

MUSIC RIDDLE

Answer on p. 160

UNIT 19: REVIEW #3
MAKE ME A MINOR

Change these major five-finger patterns into minor. Then fill in the blanks for this statement:
To turn this major five-finger pattern into a minor five-finger pattern, I changed the . . .

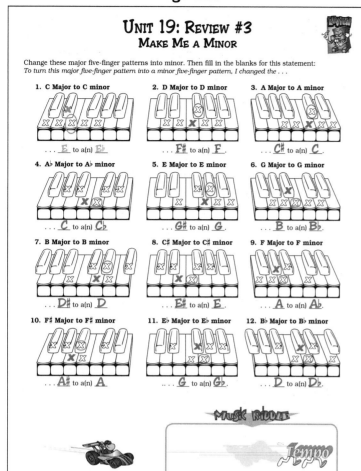

1. C Major to C minor
. . . E to a(n) Eb

2. D Major to D minor
. . . F# to a(n) F

3. A Major to A minor
. . . C# to a(n) C

4. Ab Major to Ab minor
. . . C to a(n) Cb

5. E Major to E minor
. . . G# to a(n) G

6. G Major to G minor
. . . B to a(n) Bb

7. B Major to B minor
. . . D# to a(n) D

8. C# Major to C# minor
. . . E# to a(n) E

9. F Major to F minor
. . . A to a(n) Ab

10. F# Major to F# minor
. . . A# to a(n) A

11. Eb Major to Eb minor
. . . G to a(n) Gb

12. Bb Major to Bb minor
. . . D to a(n) Db

MUSIC RIDDLE

Answer on p. 160

ALIENS WANT TO KNOW

Aliens are studying the human race and its extraordinary love for music. Currently, they are learning about **minor** five-finger patterns. They used their alien powers to transfer the names of the notes of the minor five-finger patterns to their alien fingers . . . but something went wrong, and only the 3rds transferred. Help them out by filling in the rest of the note names.

AMAZING THIRDS MARBLE MAZE

Track the marbles through the maze. There are five exits. Mark each exit with the name of the path which is exiting as follows: **M3** (Major 3rds only), **m3** (minor 3rds only), **M3/m3** (alternating Major and minor 3rds) or **N** (no paths exit here).

M3
Move through the maze using only Major 3rds (ascending or descending).

m3
Move through the maze using only minor 3rds (ascending or descending).

M3/m3
Move through the maze using alternating Major and minor 3rds (ascending or descending).

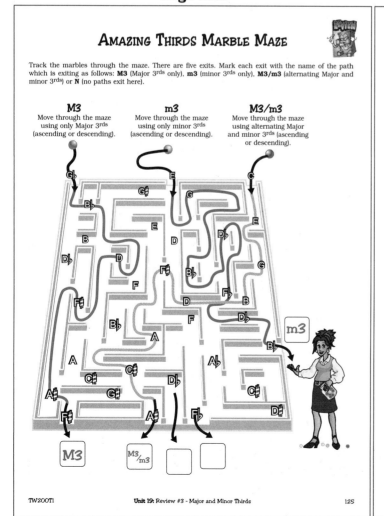

TUBING AT MINOR WATER PARK

While tubing at Minor Water Park, these nine minor triad tubing groups broke loose and were scrambled. Help each group captain (the root) find their tubing buddies (the 3rd and the 5th). Color the three tubes of each group together, using a different color for each tubing group.

Answers may vary.

YELLOW   ORANGE   RED   PURPLE   BLUE   GREEN   BROWN   LT. GREEN

MINOR I CHORDS

Major or Minor?

A. Indicate which 3rd is the Major 3rd (M3 – 4 half steps) and which is the minor 3rd (m3 – 3 half steps) for the triads below.

Just a reminder: Major triads are built with a M3 on the bottom and a m3 on the top.

If the M3 is on the bottom, it is a major triad. If the m3 is on the bottom, it is a minor triad.

Minor triads are built with a m3 on the bottom and a M3 on top.

B. Circle the third of each chord. Change these Major I chords to minor i chords by marking the lowered third with an X. Complete the statements below each keyboard.

1. The Major 3rd was *C* to *E*
   The minor 3rd is *C* to *E♭*
2. The Major 3rd was *D* to *F♯*
   The minor 3rd is *D* to *F*
3. The Major 3rd was *A* to *C♯*
   The minor 3rd is *A* to *C*
4. The Major 3rd was *A♭* to *C*
   The minor 3rd is *A♭* to *C♭*
5. The Major 3rd was *E* to *G♯*
   The minor 3rd is *E* to *G*
6. The Major 3rd was *G* to *B*
   The minor 3rd is *G* to *B♭*
7. The Major 3rd was *B* to *D♯*
   The minor 3rd is *B* to *D*
8. The Major 3rd was *E♭* to *G*
   The minor 3rd is *E♭* to *G♭*
9. The Major 3rd was *F* to *A*
   The minor 3rd is *F* to *A♭*

The Triad Path

Shade only blocks that touch (up, down, or diagonally) which are answers to the Key below.

KEY

1. Root of B♭M
2. 3rd of CM
3. 5th of Dm
4. Root of F♯M
5. 3rd of C♯m
6. 3rd of E♭m
7. 5th of B♭M
8. Root of Am
9. 3rd of B♭m
10. 3rd of D♭M
11. 5th of AM
12. 3rd of E♭M
13. 5th of F♯m
14. Root of D♭M
15. 5th of C♯m
16. 3rd of GM
17. 3rd of Em
18. 5th of Am
19. Root of Bm
20. 3rd of Fm

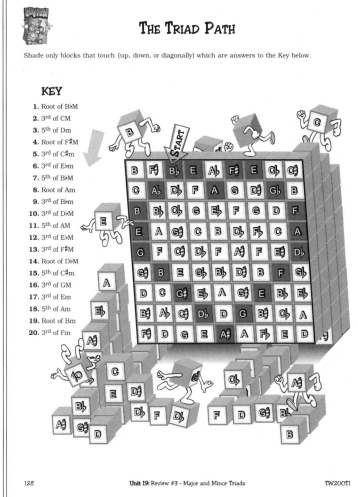

On My Terms or Yours?

Write the correct term or sign beside each definition. Then find and circle each term (up, down, across, or backward) in the puzzle below. The first one has been done as an example.

1. Soft   *piano*
2. Moderately soft
3. Moderately loud
4. Loud
5. Quickly or "running tempo"
6. "Walking tempo"
7. Gradually louder
8. Gradually softer
9. Emphasized
10. A sudden accent placed on a single note or chord
11. Gradually slowing
12. Gradually increase the tempo
13. Hold longer than its value
14. The Italian word for "end"
15. Return to the beginning of the piece and play until you reach the *fine*.
16. Markings that indicate how a note is to be played
17. The markings that indicate the volume of the music
18. The speed or pace of the music
19. Short and detached
20. Play smooth and connected
21. A curved line extended over or under two or more notes that indicate that the notes should be played legato.
22. A curved line joining two notes of the same pitch. The second note is not played but its value is added to the first note.
23. Raise the note one half step
24. Lower the note one half step
25. Cancel the sharp or flat

The names of five famous composers are also hidden: Bach, Mozart, Haydn, Beethoven and Liszt. Can you find them?

Do You Belong to the P. I. Hall of Fame?

You are a world famous private investigator. Your mission is to find and define the music terms and signs in the example below. In addition, you must circle and number the following items:

1. half step   2. whole step   3. 3rd   4. 4th   5. 5th
6. 6th   7. dotted quarter note   8. octave (8ve)
9. A minor five-finger pattern   10. D Major I chord

Each item you find is worth 10 points.

Are you Hall-of-Fame material, or are you a music detective extraordinaire?

Music Detectives Hall of Fame	
	RECORD
Linda Legato	550
Frank Fermata	520
Sammy Sharp	580
(your name)	
Music Detective Extraordinaire (600+)	
Hazel Halfstep	660
Zundel Shelzi	640
(your name)	

UNIT 20: LISTENING
PITCH AND MELODY

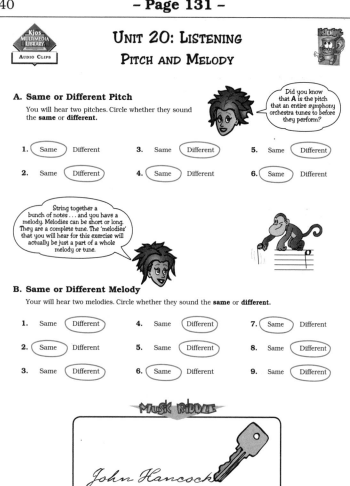

A. Same or Different Pitch

You will hear two pitches. Circle whether they sound the **same** or **different**.

1. (Same) Different   3. Same (Different)   5. Same (Different)

2. Same (Different)   4. (Same) Different   6. (Same) Different

String together a bunch of notes . . . and you have a melody. Melodies can be short or long. They are a complete tune. The 'melodies' that you will hear for this exercise will actually be just a part of a whole melody or tune.

B. Same or Different Melody

Your will hear two melodies. Circle whether they sound the **same** or **different**.

1. Same (Different)   4. Same (Different)   7. (Same) Different

2. (Same) Different   5. Same (Different)   8. Same (Different)

3. Same (Different)   6. (Same) Different   9. Same (Different)

MUSIC RIDDLE

John Hancock

Answer on p. 160

REGISTER AND DYNAMICS

A. High or Low

Listen and circle **high** or **low**.

1. (High) Low
2. High (Low)
3. High (Low)
4. (High) Low
5. High (Low)

B. Loud or Soft

Listen and circle **loud** or **soft**.

1. (Loud) Soft
2. (Loud) Soft
3. Loud (Soft)
4. (Loud) Soft
5. Loud (Soft)

C. High or Low/Loud or Soft

Mark the two boxes that best describe the melody you hear.

#	High/Low	Loud/Soft
1.	(High) Low	Loud (Soft)
2.	(High) Low	(Loud) Soft
3.	(High) Low	Loud (Soft)
4.	(High) Low	Loud (Soft)
5.	(High) Low	Loud (Soft)
6.	High (Low)	(Loud) Soft
7.	High (Low)	Loud (Soft)
8.	High (Low)	(Loud) Soft
9.	(High) Low	Loud (Soft)
10.	High (Low)	(Loud) Soft
11.	(High) Low	Loud (Soft)
12.	(High) Low	Loud (Soft)

TEMPO

A. Slow or Fast

Circle the word that best describes the tempo you hear.

1. (Slow) Fast
2. Slow (Fast)
3. (Slow) Fast
4. Slow (Fast)

B. Steady or Unsteady

Circle the word that best describes the rhythm you are hearing.

1. (Steady) Unsteady   4. Steady (Unsteady)
2. Steady (Unsteady)   5. Steady (Unsteady)
3. (Steady) Unsteady   6. Steady (Unsteady)

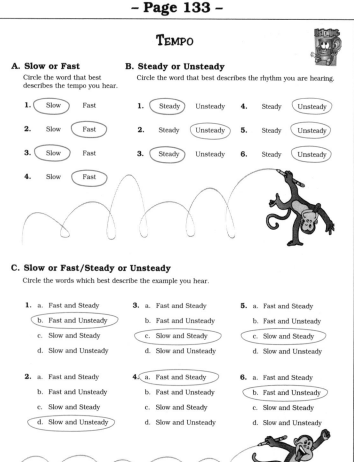

C. Slow or Fast/Steady or Unsteady

Circle the words which best describe the example you hear.

1. a. Fast and Steady
   (b. Fast and Unsteady)
   c. Slow and Steady
   d. Slow and Unsteady

2. a. Fast and Steady
   b. Fast and Unsteady
   c. Slow and Steady
   (d. Slow and Unsteady)

3. a. Fast and Steady
   b. Fast and Unsteady
   (c. Slow and Steady)
   d. Slow and Unsteady

4. (a. Fast and Steady)
   b. Fast and Unsteady
   c. Slow and Steady
   d. Slow and Unsteady

5. a. Fast and Steady
   b. Fast and Unsteady
   (c. Slow and Steady)
   d. Slow and Unsteady

6. a. Fast and Steady
   (b. Fast and Unsteady)
   c. Slow and Steady
   d. Slow and Unsteady

CRESCENDO AND DECRESCENDO

A. Crescendo or Decrescendo (Diminuendo)

Listen to each example and circle the correct answer.

1.   2.   3.   4.

B. Ascending or Descending

Circle the **A** if you hear ascending notes.
Circle the **D** if you hear descending notes.

1. A (D)   2. (A) D

3. (A) D   4. (A) D

C. Ascending or Descending/Crescendo or Decrescendo

For each example, mark the picture that best describes the sound you hear.

1.   2.   3.

4.   5.   6.

STEPS AND SKIPS

A. Steps or Skips

Listen to the example of notes moving by steps or skips. Mark the box that best describes what you hear.

1. Steps | Skips   4. Steps | Skips
2. Steps | Skips   5. Steps | Skips
3. Steps | Skips   6. Steps | Skips

B. Steps or Skips/Crescendo or Decrescendo

Mark one box that best describes the example you hear.

 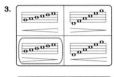 

1.   3.
2.   4.
5.   6.

MAJOR AND MINOR

A. Major or Minor Five-Finger Pattern

Identify the five-finger pattern you hear as Major or minor. Circle your answer.

1. Major (minor)   5. (Major) minor   9. Major (minor)
2. (Major) minor   6. Major (minor)   10. (Major) minor
3. Major (minor)   7. Major (minor)   11. (Major) minor
4. (Major) (minor)   8. (Major) (minor)   12. (Major) (minor)

B. Major or Minor Third

Identify the third you hear as Major or minor. Circle your answer.

1. (Major) minor   5. (Major) minor   9. (Major) minor
2. Major (minor)   6. Major (minor)   10. Major (minor)
3. Major (minor)   7. (Major) minor   11. Major (minor)
4. (Major) (minor)   8. (Major) (minor)   12. (Major) minor

C. Major or Minor I (i) Chord

Identify the chord you hear as Major or minor. Circle your answer.

1. (Major) minor   5. (Major) minor   9. (Major) minor
2. (Major) minor   6. (Major) minor   10. (Major) minor
3. (Major) minor   7. Major (minor)   11. Major (minor)
4. Major (minor)   8. (Major) minor   12. (Major) minor

INTERVALS IN A MAJOR FIVE-FINGER PATTERN

Think about the intervals you might hear using the notes of a major five-finger pattern. The largest interval you could make would be a perfect 5th!

Always think of the lowest note in the interval as the first note of the pattern, and then count up from there using the notes of that five-finger pattern.

Intervals in the C Major five-finger pattern:

P1 M2 M3 P4 P5
(unison)

Remember to add the sharps or flats that belong to the five-finger pattern you are using to build each interval.

In the box below each example, identify the interval you hear and circle the second note that completes that interval. The first one has been done as an example.

1. B five-finger pattern: P4
2. D five-finger pattern: M3
3. E five-finger pattern: P5
4. A five-finger pattern: M2
5. F five-finger pattern: M3
6. F# five-finger pattern: P5
7. C# five-finger pattern: M3
8. Bb five-finger pattern: P4
9. Ab five-finger pattern: M2
10. G five-finger pattern: P1
11. Gb five-finger pattern: M3
12. Db five-finger pattern: P5

TWO WAYS TO HEAR MAJOR AND PERFECT INTERVALS

When you hear an interval, you can "fill in" the notes in between in your mind to help identify it.

These are major and perfect intervals, so remember to think of the first note of the major five-finger pattern and add the appropriate sharp or flat.

M3

A. Using the Five-Finger Pattern

Identify the interval in the box and draw the second note you hear on the staff.

1. P5   2. M2   3. P4   4. P1   5. M3   6. P4
7. M3   8. P4   9. M2   10. P4   11. M3   12. M2

To help me hear intervals quickly, I think of a song that begins with that interval. For example, the first two notes of "Are You Sleeping" make a M2. The first two notes of "The Bear Went Over the Mountain" make a M3.

Use these tunes, or find your own. Choose tunes that you know really well and can remember quickly.

P1 Yankee Doodle (same note)
M2 Are You Sleeping?
M3 The Bear Went Over the Mountain
P4 The Farmer in the Dell
P5 Twinkle, Twinkle (2nd two notes)

B. Thinking of a Song

Circle the interval you hear.

1. M3 (P4)   7. M2 P1 (M3)   13. P5 (P4) P1 M2   19. P1 M2 (M3) P4 P5
2. (M2) P5   8. P5 M3 (P4)   14. (M3) P5 P1 M2   20. (P1) M2 M3 P4 P5
3. P5 (P1)   9. (M2) P1 M3   15. (M2) M3 P4 P5   21. P1 M2 M3 (P4) P5
4. M2 (M3)   10. (M2) P1 M3   16. P1 (M3) M2 P4   22. P1 M2 M3 (P4) P5
5. P4 (M3)   11. (P5) M3 P4   17. M2 M3 P4 (P5)   23. P1 (M2) M3 P4 P5
6. M3 (P5)   12. M2 (P1) M3   18. P4 (M3) M2 P1   24. P1 M2 M3 (P4) P5

8THS ARE PERFECT, TOO!

An 8th (octave) is also a perfect interval. It is the same note, but an octave higher.

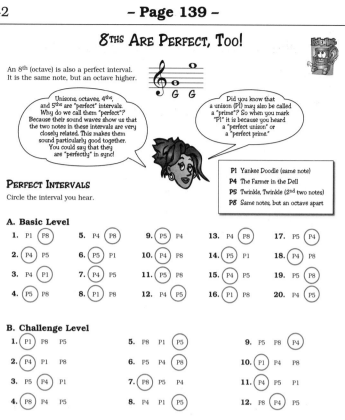

Unisons, octaves, 4ths, and 5ths are "perfect" intervals. Why do we call them "perfect"? Because their sound waves show us that the two notes in these intervals are very closely related. This makes them sound particularly good together. You could say that they are "perfectly" in sync!

Did you know that a unison (P1) may also be called a "prime"? So when you mark "P1" it is because you heard a "perfect unison" or a "perfect prime."

P1 Yankee Doodle (same note)
P4 The Farmer in the Dell
P5 Twinkle, Twinkle (2nd two notes)
P8 Same notes, but an octave apart

PERFECT INTERVALS

Circle the interval you hear.

A. Basic Level

1. P1 (P8) 5. P4 (P8) 9. (P5) P4 13. P4 (P8) 17. P5 (P4)
2. (P4) P5 6. (P5) P1 10. (P4) P8 14. (P5) P4 18. (P4) P8
3. P4 (P1) 7. (P4) P5 11. (P5) P8 15. (P4) P5 19. P5 (P8)
4. (P5) P8 8. (P1) P8 12. P4 (P5) 16. (P1) P8 20. P4 (P5)

B. Challenge Level

1. (P1) P8 P5 5. P8 (P1) P5 9. P5 P8 (P4)
2. (P4) P1 P8 6. P5 (P4) P8 10. (P1) P4 P8
3. P5 (P4) P1 7. (P8) P5 P4 11. (P4) P5 P1
4. (P8) P4 P5 8. P4 P1 (P5) 12. P8 (P4) P5

C. Genius Level

1. P1 (P4) P5 P8 5. P1 (P4) P5 P8 9. P1 P4 P5 (P8)
2. P1 P4 P5 (P8) 6. P1 (P4) P5 P8 10. P1 P4 (P5) P8
3. P1 P4 (P5) P8 7. P1 P4 P5 (P8) 11. (P1) P4 P5 P8
4. (P1) P4 P5 P8 8. P1 (P4) P5 P8 12. P1 P4 P5 (P8)

TWO MORE MAJOR INTERVALS

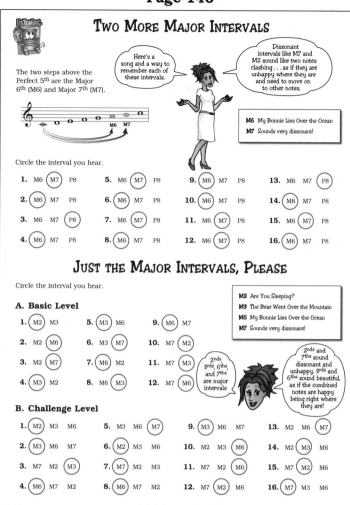

The two steps above the Perfect 5th are the Major 6th (M6) and Major 7th (M7).

Here's a song and a way to remember each of these intervals.

Dissonant intervals like M7 and M2 sound like two notes clashing . . . as if they are unhappy where they are and need to move on to other notes.

M6 My Bonnie Lies Over the Ocean
M7 Sounds very dissonant!

Circle the interval you hear.

1. M6 (M7) P8 5. M6 (M7) P8 9. (M6) M7 P8 13. M6 M7 (P8)
2. (M6) M7 P8 6. (M6) M7 P8 10. (M6) M7 P8 14. (M6) M7 P8
3. M6 (M7) P8 7. M6 (M7) P8 11. M6 (M7) P8 15. M6 (M7) P8
4. (M6) M7 P8 8. (M6) M7 P8 12. M6 (M7) P8 16. (M6) M7 P8

JUST THE MAJOR INTERVALS, PLEASE

Circle the interval you hear.

M2 Are You Sleeping?
M3 The Bear Went Over the Mountain
M6 My Bonnie Lies Over the Ocean
M7 Sounds very dissonant!

A. Basic Level

1. (M2) M3 5. (M3) M6 9. (M6) M7
2. M2 (M6) 6. M3 (M7) 10. M7 (M2)
3. M2 (M7) 7. (M6) M2 11. M7 (M2)
4. (M3) M2 8. M6 (M3) 12. M7 (M6)

B. Challenge Level

1. (M2) M3 M6 5. M3 M6 (M7) 9. (M3) M6 M7 13. M2 M6 (M7)
2. (M3) M6 M7 6. (M2) M3 M6 10. M2 M3 (M6) 14. M2 (M3) M6
3. M7 M2 (M3) 7. (M7) M2 M3 11. M7 M2 (M6) 15. M7 (M2) M6
4. (M6) M7 M2 8. (M6) M2 M3 12. M7 (M2) M6 16. (M7) M3 M6

2nds, 3rds, 6ths, and 7ths are major intervals

2nds and 7ths sound dissonant and unhappy. 3rds and 6ths sound beautiful, as if the combined notes are happy being right where they are!

MORE INTERVAL IDENTIFICATION

JUST THE MAJOR INTERVALS (CONT.)

C. Genius Level

1. M2 (M3) M6 M7 5. M2 (M3) M6 M7 9. M2 (M3) M6 M7
2. (M2) M3 M6 M7 6. M2 M3 M6 (M7) 10. M2 M3 M6 (M7)
3. M2 M3 (M6) M7 7. (M2) M3 M6 M7 11. M2 M3 M6 (M7)
4. M2 M3 M6 (M7) 8. M2 M3 (M6) M7 12. (M2) M3 M6 M7

ALL THE INTERVALS OF A MAJOR SCALE

Circle the interval you hear.

P1 Yankee Doodle (same note)
M2 Are You Sleeping?
M3 The Bear Went Over the Mountain
P4 The Farmer in the Dell
P5 Twinkle, Twinkle (2nd two notes)
M6 My Bonnie Lies Over the Ocean
M7 Sounds very dissonant!
P8 Same notes, but an octave apart

1. M2 M3 (P5) P8 13. M2 M3 P5 (M7) P8
2. P1 (P4) M6 M7 14. (P1) P4 P5 M6 M7
3. M2 M3 P4 (P8) 15. M2 M3 P4 (M6) P8
4. P1 (M2) P5 M6 16. P1 M2 (P4) P5 M6
5. M2 (M3) P5 P8 17. M2 (M3) P5 M7 P8
6. (P1) P4 M7 P8 18. M2 M3 P4 (M6) M7
7. M2 M3 P4 (M7) 19. (M2) M3 P4 M6 P8
8. P1 M2 P4 (P5) 20. P1 M2 P4 P5 (M6)
9. P1 P4 (M6) M7 21. P1 P4 P5 (M6) M7
10. M2 (M3) P4 P8 22. M2 (M3) P4 M6 P8
11. (M6) M2 P5 P1 23. P1 M2 (P5) M6 M7
12. (M2) M3 P8 P5 24. M2 M3 (P5) M6 P8

MUSIK RIDDLE

Answer on p. 160

MAJOR AND PERFECT INTERVALS

A. Identify the intervals, then circle the one you hear.

1. (P5) M6 3. M2 (P1) 5. (M2) P4
2. (P4) M7 4. (P8) M6 6. (M6) P5

B. Identify the intervals, then circle the one you hear.

1. M2 (M7) P4 4. M7 (P4) P1
2. (M5) M7 P1 5. P5 (M3) P4
3. (M3) P5 M2 6. P8 (M7) M6

C. Identify the intervals, then circle the one you hear.

1. M2 (M7) P4 P5
2. M6 M7 P1 (M3)
3. M3 P5 M2 (P4)
4. (M6) P4 P1 M2
5. P8 M3 (M6) P4
6. P8 M7 M6 (P5)

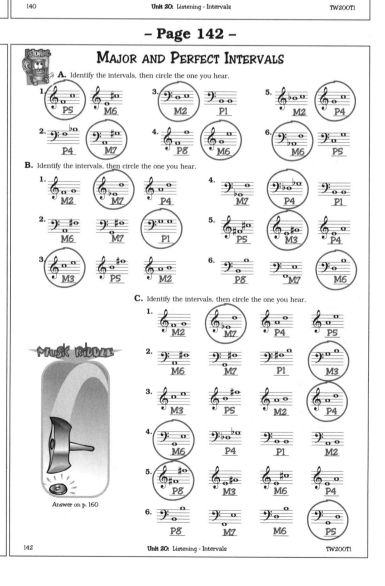

MUSIK RIDDLE

Answer on p. 160

SAME OR DIFFERENT RHYTHM?

You will hear two rhythms. Determine if the second rhythm you hear is the same or different from the first. Circle the **second** rhythm you hear. Remember to feel the eighth notes internally.

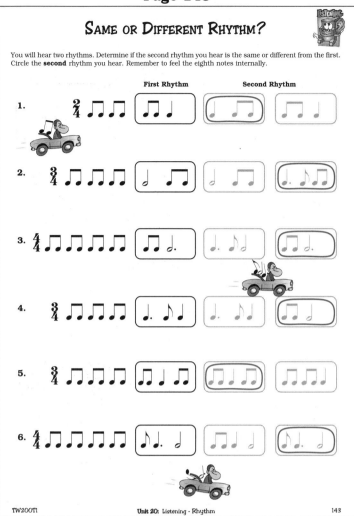

WILL THE REAL RHYTHM PLEASE STAND UP?

A. Circle the one-measure rhythm you hear. Remember to feel the eighth notes internally.

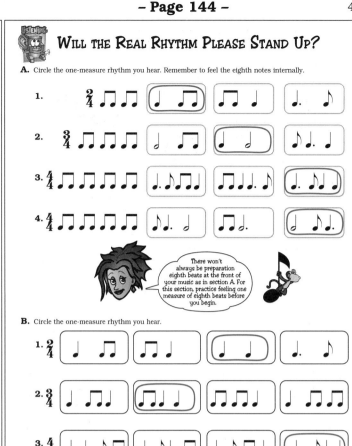

B. Circle the one-measure rhythm you hear.

RHYTHMIC DICTATION #1

Follow these steps when taking rhythmic dictation:

1. The eighth notes for one measure of each time signature are written. As you listen to each example, follow along by counting out loud and pointing to each eighth note.

2. When you hear a note, draw a line through the eighth note you are pointing to.

3. Draw the note values to match the rhythm that you marked.

RHYTHMIC DICTATION #2

As you listen to each example, follow along by counting out loud and pointing to each eighth note. When you hear a note, draw a line through the eighth note you are pointing to. In the box beside each example, draw note values to match the rhythm you marked,

A. Rhythmic Dictation in 2/4 Time

B. Rhythmic Dictation in 3/4 Time

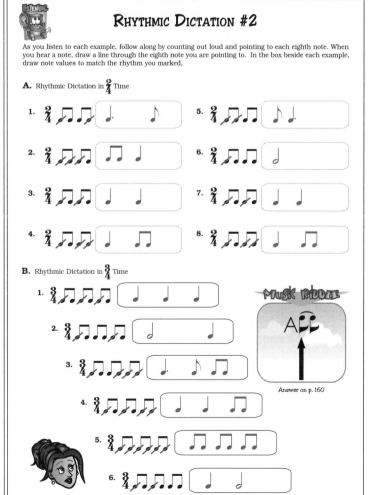

Answer on p. 160

RHYTHMIC DICTATION #3

As you listen to each example, follow along by counting out loud and pointing to each eighth note. When you hear a note played, draw a line through the eighth note you are pointing to. In the box beside each example. draw note values to match the rhythm you marked,

A. Rhythmic Dictation in 2/4 Time

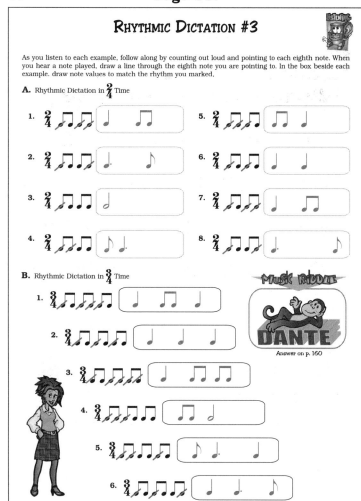

B. Rhythmic Dictation in 3/4 Time

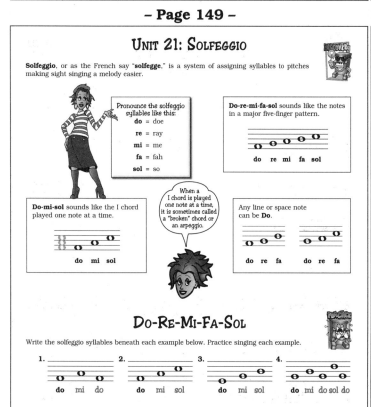

MUSIC RIDDLE

DANTE

Answer on p. 160

Unit 20: Listening - Rhythm

RHYTHMIC DICTATION #4

As you listen to each example, follow along by counting out loud and pointing to each eighth note. When you hear a note played, draw a line through the eighth note you are pointing to. In the box beside each example, draw note values to match the rhythm you marked,

Rhythmic Dictation in 4/4 Time

Unit 20: Listening - Rhythm

UNIT 21: SOLFEGGIO

Solfeggio, or as the French say "**solfegge**," is a system of assigning syllables to pitches making sight singing a melody easier.

Pronounce the solfeggio syllables like this:
do = doe
re = ray
mi = me
fa = fah
sol = so

Do-re-mi-fa-sol sounds like the notes in a major five-finger pattern.

do re mi fa sol

Do-mi-sol sounds like the I chord played one note at a time.

do mi sol

When a I chord is played one note at a time, it is sometimes called a "broken" chord or an arpeggio.

Any line or space note can be **Do**.

do re fa   do re fa

DO-RE-MI-FA-SOL

Write the solfeggio syllables beneath each example below. Practice singing each example.

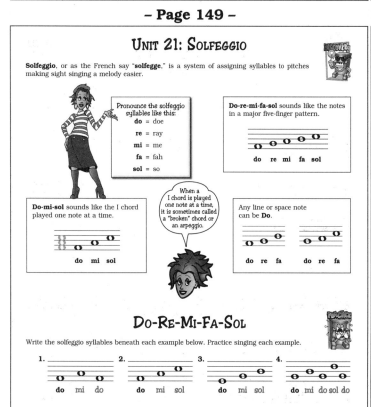

1. do mi do
2. do mi sol
3. do mi sol
4. do mi do sol do

5. do re fa fa mi
6. mi do mi re do
7. sol do sol fa mi

8. do mi sol fa mi re mi fa sol do sol do

Unit 21: Solfeggio

MORE SINGING WITH SOLFEGGIO

A. Write the solfeggio syllables beneath each example below. Practice singing each example.

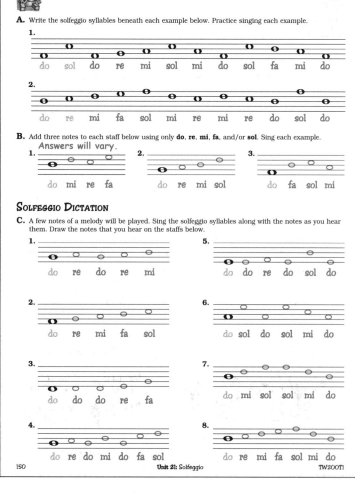

1. do sol do re mi sol mi do sol fa mi do

2. do re mi fa sol mi re mi re do sol do

B. Add three notes to each staff below using only **do**, **re**, **mi**, **fa**, and/or **sol**. Sing each example.

Answers will vary.

1. do mi re fa
2. do re mi sol
3. do fa sol mi

SOLFEGGIO DICTATION

C. A few notes of a melody will be played. Sing the solfeggio syllables along with the notes as you hear them. Draw the notes that you hear on the staffs below.

1. do re do re mi
2. do re mi fa sol
3. do do do re fa
4. do re do mi do fa sol

5. do do re do sol do
6. do sol do sol mi do
7. do mi sol sol mi do
8. do re mi fa sol mi do

Unit 21: Solfeggio

SOLFEGGIO IN HARMONY

Find a partner and sing these tunes using solfeggio syllables.

Hot Cross Buns

Hush-A-Bye

Mary Had a Little Lamb

TW200T1   **Unit 21:** Solfeggio   151

WHERE'S THE "DO"?

A. These songs do not begin on **do**. Determine which solfeggio syllable they begin on and write the solfeggio syllable beneath each note. Now sing the songs. Can you name any of them?

B. C is "do" in each of the following riddles. To solve the riddles, write in each note's solfeggio syllable.

152   **Unit 21:** Solfeggio   TW200T1

BE A MOZART MILLIONAIRE!

Answer all the questions. Have your teacher correct your work. Your score depends on how far you answered the questions correctly (i.e., If you answered the $100-$16,000 questions correctly, but missed the $32,000 question, your score is $16,000.)

For **$100**   Where was Mozart born? <u>Austria</u>

For **$500**   What was Mozart's sister's nickname? <u>Nannerl</u>

For **$1000**   How old was Mozart when he wrote his first composition? <u>5</u>

For **$2000**   Name three unusual feats Mozart could perform for royalty. <u>Playing with a cloth over the keyboard, playing blindfolded, naming notes without looking</u>

For **$4000**   Who made most of Mozart's decisions for him? <u>his father</u>

For **$8000**   Name two instruments Mozart could play. <u>harpsichord, violin</u>

For **$16,000**   For whom did Mozart play when he toured Europe and Britain? <u>royalty</u>

For **$32,000**   How many pieces did Mozart write in his lifetime? <u>600+</u>

For **$64,000**   How old was Mozart when he died? <u>35</u>

For **$125,000**   What was unfortunate about Mozart's burial? <u>buried in pauper's grave</u>

For **$500,000**   Describe how Mozart composed. <u>in his head while in bed in carriages and then wrote when he could</u>

For **$1,000,000**   Did Mozart practice on the piano or clavier when he was young? <u>clavier</u>

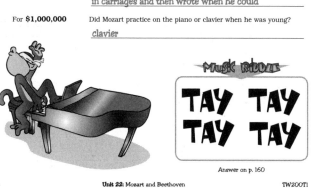

MUSIC RIDDLE

TAY TAY
TAY TAY

Answer on p. 160

154   **Unit 22:** Mozart and Beethoven   TW200T1

RONDO ALLA TURCA

Listen to Mozart's *Rondo Alla Turca*. Mark the repetitions in blue and sequences in red.

TW200T1   **Unit 22:** Mozart and Beethoven   155

At the end of the concert, the audience gave Beethoven standing ovations, but he did not hear them and did not see them standing. One of the soloists took the composer's hand and turned him to face the audience. The whole audience erupted. There were handkerchiefs in the air, hats and raised hands so that Beethoven could see the ovation. The theatre house had never seen such enthusiastic applause! In fact, it was customary for the king and queen to be greeted with three ovations as they entered the hall. Beethoven received five at the end of the performance! This was unheard of and the police had to break off this spontaneous explosion of ovations. Beethoven left the concert deeply grateful for the audience's appreciation.

On a dark and cloudy day three years later, Beethoven lay on his bed. In the afternoon came a terrible storm. Thunder made the room shudder. Beethoven opened his eyes and raised his right arm towards the sky with his fist clenched. Then his hand fell to the ground. His eyes closed. Beethoven died at age 56.

Beethoven's music is grand in many ways. His music ranges from very soft to extremely loud. He used more lower and higher keys on the piano than any composer before him. He added instruments to the orchestra for the largest orchestra up to that time. He composed a symphony that included a large chorus of singers as well as all the instruments. He was one of the greatest composers to have ever lived!

Complete the Beethoven timeline by filling in the letters of the events.

Beethoven Timeline

Events

A. First signs of deafness appear.

B. 20,000 people came to his funeral

C. Played and improvised for Mozart.

D. Was given five standing ovations at the first performance of the Ninth Symphony.

E. Met with Haydn for the last time.

F. Gave his first concert at the age of 7.

Letter	Year	Event
	1770	Born in Bonn, Germany / Took music lessons from his father
F	1777	
C	1778	Could play violin, viola, organ and piano
	1787	
A	1793	Becomes a student of Haydn. / Played in piano competitions in Vienna.
E	1797	
	1808	
	1811	Wrote Für Elise.
D	1811	Played his fifth piano concerto in his last public performance.
B	1823	
	1827	Died on a stormy, snowy afternoon.

Für Elise or Therese?

There is a story about the famous piece Für Elise that may or may not be true. When Beethoven was forty years old he fell in love with a student—the beautiful eighteen-year-old Therese Malfatti. He was invited to the Malfatti household for a party thrown by Therese's father. Beethoven composed a piece especially for Therese and he planned to propose to her on that night. As the night progressed he became so nervous that he was unable to play the piece or propose. All he could do was write Therese's name on the music, but very poorly. After Therese died, the manuscript was found among her things. A publisher recognized the handwriting as Beethoven's and published the work. But since the writing was so bad it was mistakenly read as "Fur Elise" and has been known by that name ever since.

Reconstruct this music to be the theme of the famous piece "Für Elise" by Beethoven. Number your choices in order from 1 through 7.

Answers 2 and 5 are interchangeable.

AUDIO CLIPS

Kjos MULTIMEDIA LIBRARY

The following listening examples (for use with corresponding pages of the student workbook) are also available online as audio clips at *www.kjos. com*. These recordings are professionally produced using a variety of music instrument sounds. They are valuable for independent student work wherever a student has access to the internet. To find these recordings, go to *www. kjos.com*, click on the Kjos Multimedia Library icon and then "Theory."

Accelerando 1 Listening Section Music Examples

Based on page numbers of the Accelerando 1 theory book.

(See previous page for information about free recordings available on-line.)

Unit 20: Listening

Page 131A: *Pitch: Same or Different*

Page 131B: *Melody: Same or Different*

48

Page 132C: *High or Low/Loud or Soft*

Page 133A: *Slow or Fast*

50

Page 133B: *Steady or Unsteady*

Example 1: Play Steady   *Example 2: Play Unsteady*

Example 3: Play Steady

Example 4: Play Unsteady

Example 5: Play Unsteady

Example 6: Play Unsteady

Page 133C: *Slow or Fast/Steady or Unsteady*

Example 1: Play Fast and Unsteady

Example 2: Play Slow and Unsteady

Example 3: Play Slow and Steady

Example 4: Play Fast and Steady

Example 5: Play Slow and Steady

Example 6: Play Fast and Unsteady

Page 134A: *Crescendo or Decrescendo*

Example 1   *Example 2*

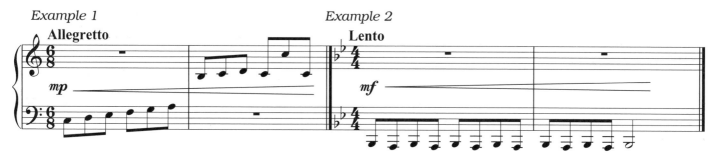

52

Example 3

Example 4

Page 134B: *Ascending or Descending*

Example 1

Example 2

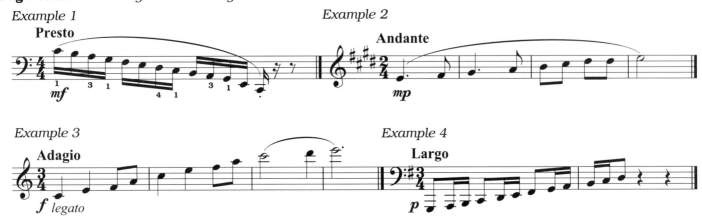

Example 3

Example 4

Page 134C: *Ascending or Descending/Crescendo or Decrescendo*

Example 1

Example 2

Example 3

Example 4

Example 5

Example 6

Page 135A: *Steps or Skips*

Example 1

Example 2

Example 3

Example 4   Example 5   Example 6

Page 135B: *Steps or Skips/Crescendo or Decrescendo*

Example 1   Example 2

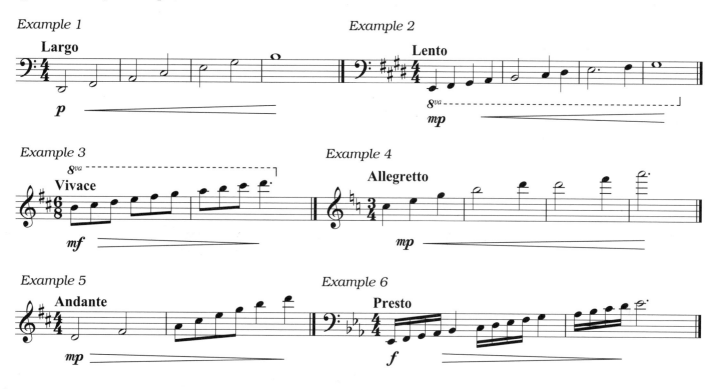

Example 3   Example 4

Example 5   Example 6

Page 136A: *Major or Minor Five-Finger Pattern*

Example 1   Example 2   Example 3   Example 4

Example 5   Example 6   Example 7   Example 8

Example 9   Example 10   Example 11   Example 12

Page 136B: *Major or Minor Third*

Page 136C: *Major or Minor I (i) Chord*

Page 137: *Intervals in a Major Five-Finger Pattern*

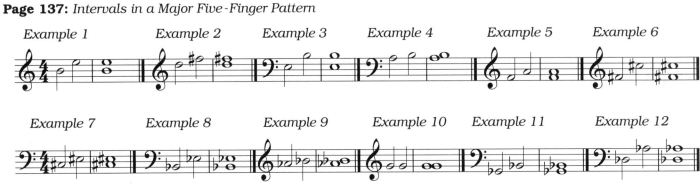

Page 138A: *Identify Major and Perfect Intervals (Using the Five-Finger Pattern)*

Page 138B: *Identify Major and Perfect Intervals (Thinking of a Song)*

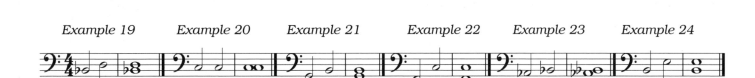

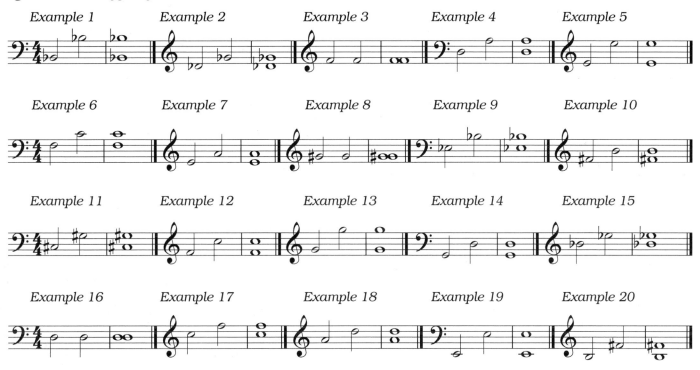

Page 139A: *Identify Perfect Intervals – Basic Level*

Page 139B: *Identify Perfect Intervals – Challenge Level*

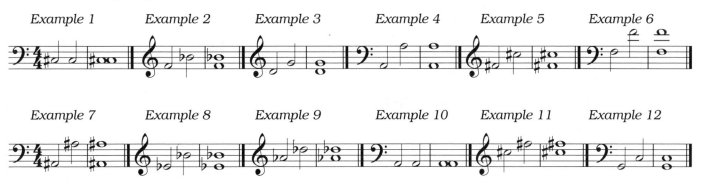

56

Page 139C: *Identify Perfect Intervals – Genius Level*

Page 140: *Two More Major Intervals*

Page 140A: *Just the Major Intervals – Basic Level*

Page 140B: *Just the Major Intervals – Challenge Level*

Page 141C: *Just the Major Intervals – Genius Level*

Page 141: *Identify All the Intervals of the Major Scale*

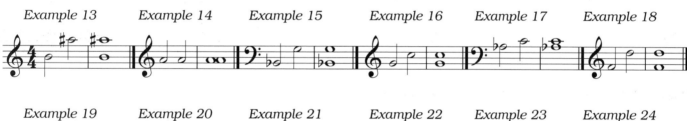

Page 142A: *Identify the Major and Perfect Intervals*

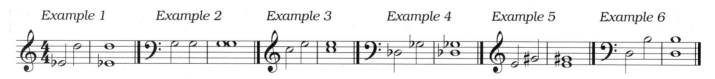

Page 142B: *Identify the Major and Perfect Intervals*

Page 142C: *Identify the Major and Perfect Intervals*

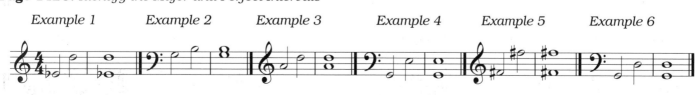

58

Page 143: *Same or Different Rhythm?*

Page 147B: *Rhythmic Dictation #3*

Page 148: *Rhythmic Dictation #4*

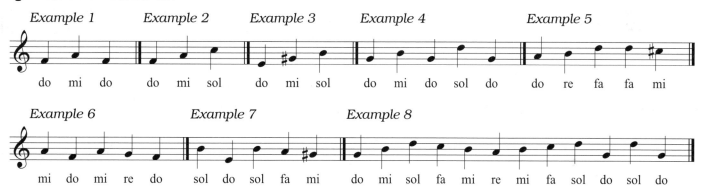

Unit 21: Solfeggio

Page 149: *Do-Re-Mi-Fa-Sol*

Page 150A: *More Singing with Solfeggio*

Page 150C: *Solfeggio Dictation*

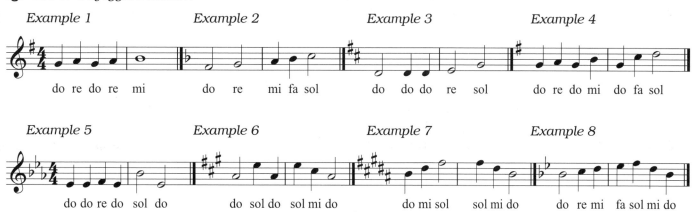

This page is left blank intentionally.

Keyboard Gymnastics®

Name_____ **Date**_____ Score_____ /100

1. Fill in the missing letters of the music alphabet **moving forward**.   *1*

<u>A</u>   __   __   <u>D</u>   __   <u>F</u>   __   <u>A</u>

2. Fill in the missing letters of the music alphabet **moving backward**.   *1*

<u>F</u>   __   <u>A</u>   __   <u>C</u>   __   __   <u>F</u>   ⬅ START HERE

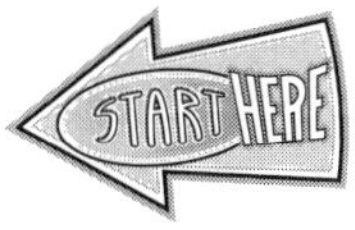

3. Write the name of each white key on the keyboard.   *1*

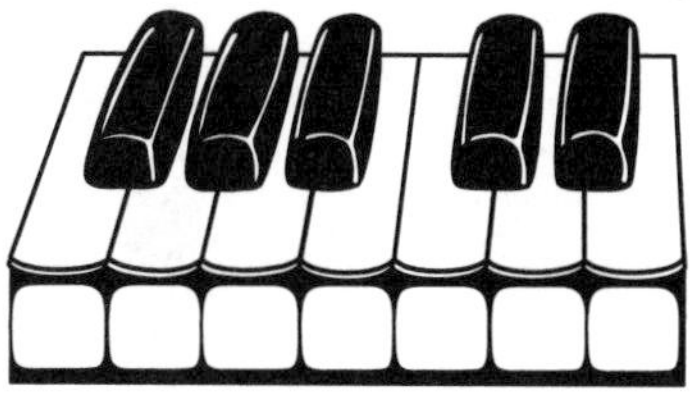

4. Write the counts beneath each note and rest in the rhythm below.   *8*

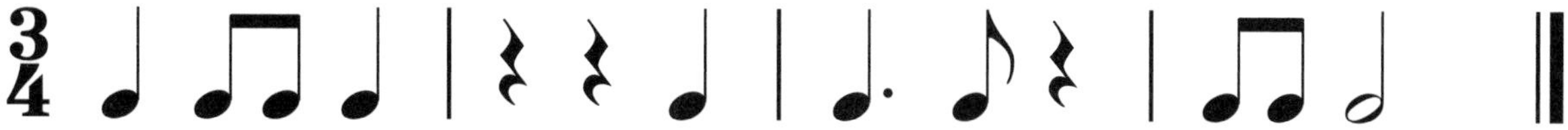

5. Draw the **brace**, **treble clef sign**, **double bar**, **repeat sign**, **barline**,   *6*
and **bass clef sign** on the grand staff below.

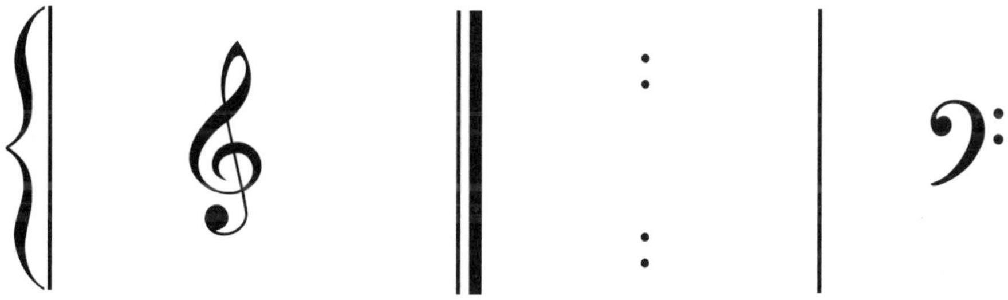

6. Name the notes in the boxes provided.

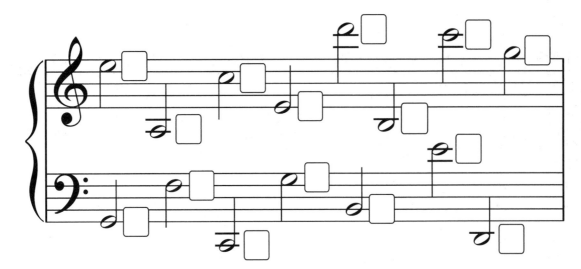

7. Write only one name for each of the shaded keys.

8. Mark the keys on the keyboard to match the notes on the staff. Decide if the notes represent a half step or whole step. **Circle your answer**.

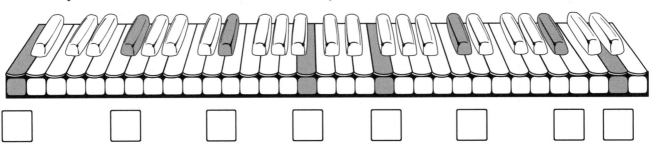

Half Step   or   Whole Step?   Half Step or Whole Step?

9. Name the intervals.

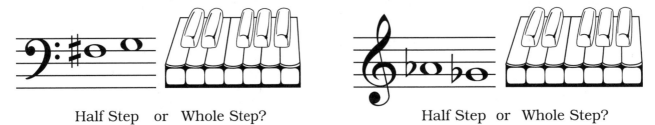

10. True or **False**. Mozart composed music when he was very young.

11. True or **False**. Beethoven was born in America.

12. Mark the keys that belong to the **Major five-finger patterns** on the keyboards below.
Using whole notes, draw the five-finger patterns and I chords on the staff. *12*

<table>
<tr><td>**F Major**
Five-Finger Pattern</td><td>**F Major**
Five-Finger Pattern</td><td>**FM**
I Chord</td></tr>
</table>

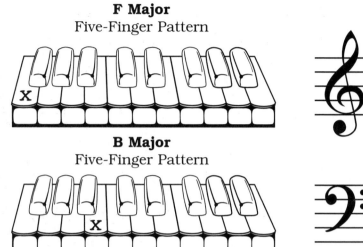

B Major
Five-Finger Pattern

B Major
Five-Finger Pattern

BM
I Chord

13. Mark the keys that belong to the **minor five-finger patterns** on the keyboards below.
Using whole notes, draw the five-finger patterns and I chords on the staff. *12*

A minor
Five-Finger Pattern

A minor
Five-Finger Pattern

Am
i Chord

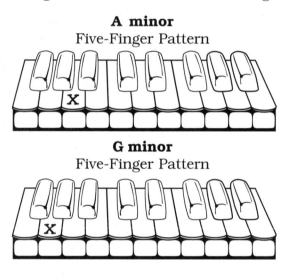
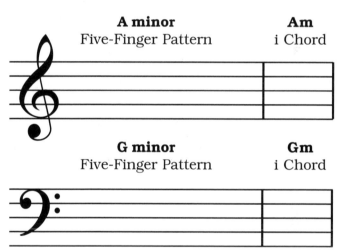

G minor
Five-Finger Pattern

G minor
Five-Finger Pattern

Gm
i Chord

14. Mark the key to complete the 3^{rds}
on the keyboards. *2*

Up a major 3rd Down a minor 3rd

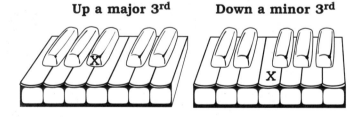

15. Draw the note to complete the 3^{rds}
on the staffs. *2*

Down a major 3rd Up a minor 3rd

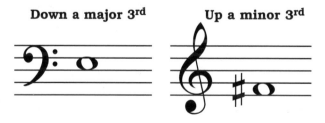

16. Mark the keys to complete the triads
on the keyboards. *4*

A Major   E♭ minor

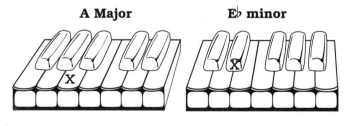

17. Draw the notes to complete the triads
on the staffs. *4*

A♭ Major   D minor

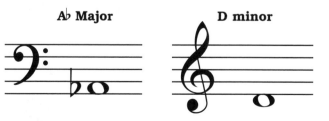

TW201T1

I'm Done Workin' on the Railroad!

Folk/arr. Lloyd

18. There are many things circled in **I'm Done Workin' on the Railroad!**
Find each sign and term listed below and write its number in the box provided.
Write the number of the matching sign by the term in the box provided.

18

Not all of the circled items will be matched below.

Crescendo	Accent	Dynamic marking that means "loud"	A whole step
Staccato	Brace	Term meaning "slow down gradually"	F Major I chord
Treble clef	Fermata	P4 (Perfect fourth)	Sequence
Tie	Decrescendo		
Natural	A dotted quarter note	Term meaning "running tempo"	Sharp

Keyboard Gymnastics®

Name_____ **K E Y** _____ Date_____ Score_____ /100

1. Fill in the missing letters of the music alphabet **moving forward**.   *1*

A   B   C   D   E   F   G   A

2. Fill in the missing letters of the music alphabet **moving backward**.   *1*

F   G   A   B   C   D   E   F

3. Write the name of each white key on the keyboard.   *1*

4. Write the counts beneath each note and rest in the rhythm below.   *8*

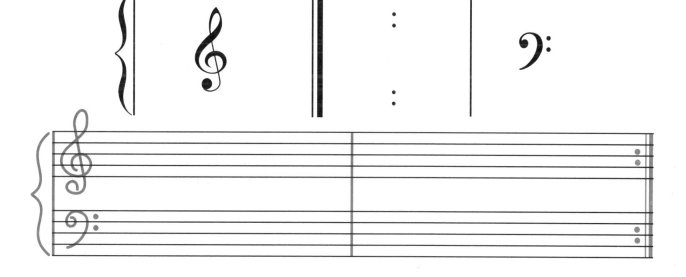

5. Draw the **brace**, **treble clef sign**, **double bar**, **repeat sign**, **barline**,   *6*
and **bass clef sign** on the grand staff below.

6. Name the notes in the boxes provided.

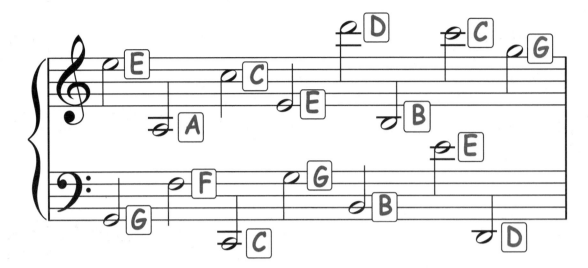

7. Write only one name for each of the shaded keys.

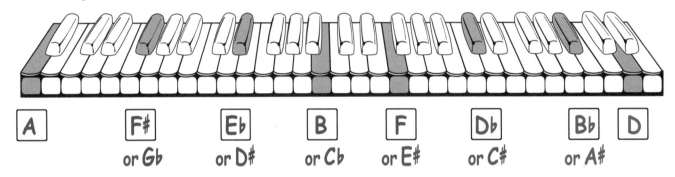

8. Mark the keys on the keyboard to match the notes on the staff. Decide if the notes represent a half step or whole step. **Circle your answer**.

9. Name the intervals.

5th   6th   2nd   3rd

10. (True) or **False**. Mozart composed music when he was very young.

11. True or (**False**.) Beethoven was born in America.

12. Mark the keys that belong to the **Major five-finger patterns** on the keyboards below.
Using whole notes, draw the five-finger patterns and I chords on the staff.   *12*

F Major
Five-Finger Pattern

F Major
Five-Finger Pattern

FM
I Chord

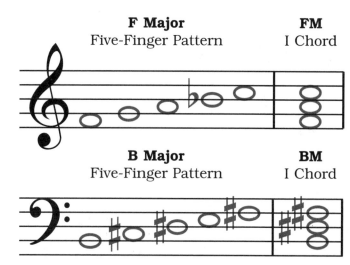

B Major
Five-Finger Pattern

B Major
Five-Finger Pattern

BM
I Chord

13. Mark the keys that belong to the **minor five-finger patterns** on the keyboards below.
Using whole notes, draw the five-finger patterns and I chords on the staff.   *12*

A minor
Five-Finger Pattern

A minor
Five-Finger Pattern

Am
i Chord

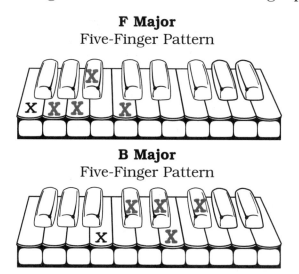

G minor
Five-Finger Pattern

G minor
Five-Finger Pattern

Gm
i Chord

14. Mark the key to complete the 3rds
on the keyboards.   *2*

15. Draw the note to complete the 3rds
on the staffs.   *2*

Up a major 3rd   **Down a minor 3rd**

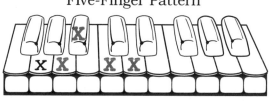

Down a major 3rd   **Up a minor 3rd**

16. Mark the keys to complete the triads
on the keyboards.   4

17. Draw the notes to complete the triads
on the staffs.   4

A Major   **E♭ minor**

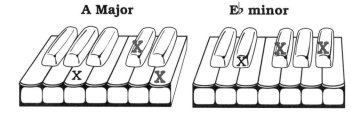

A♭ Major   **D minor**

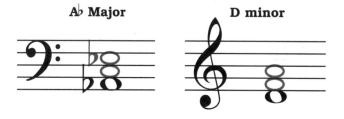

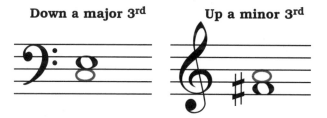
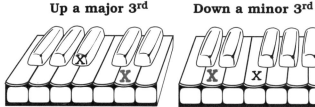
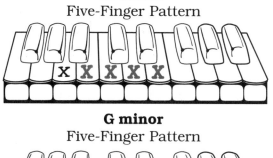

I'm Done Workin' on the Railroad!

Folk/arr. Lloyd

18. There are many things circled in **I'm Done Workin' on the Railroad!**   *18*
Find each sign and term listed below and write its number in the box provided.
Write the number of the matching sign by the term in the box provided.

Not all of the circled items will be matched below.

16 Crescendo	**19** Accent	**3** Dynamic marking that means "loud"	**18** A whole step
17 Staccato	**2** Brace	**20** Term meaning "slow down gradually"	**24** F Major I chord
8 Treble clef	**23** Fermata	**7** P4 (Perfect fourth)	**10** Sequence
9 Tie	**22** Decrescendo	**1** Term meaning "running tempo"	**13** Sharp
12 Natural	**6** A dotted quarter note		

Keyboard Gymnastics®

Ear Training Test
Level T1
(Accelerando 1)
Form A

Name____________________________ **Date**___________ Score_____ /100 ***Points***

1. Circle whether the pitches are the **same** or **different**. *8*

A. Same Different **B.** Same Different

C. Same Different **D.** Same Different

2. Circle whether the melodies sound the **same** or **different**. *8*

A. Same Different **B.** Same Different

C. Same Different **D.** Same Different

3. Mark the two boxes that best describe the example you hear. *8*

A.

High	Loud
Low	Soft

B.

High	Loud
Low	Soft

C.

High	Loud
Low	Soft

D.

High	Loud
Low	Soft

4. Circle the words that best describe the example you hear. *8*

A.
Fast and Steady
Fast and Unsteady
Slow and Steady
Slow and Unsteady

B.
Fast and Steady
Fast and Unsteady
Slow and Steady
Slow and Unsteady

C.
Fast and Steady
Fast and Unsteady
Slow and Steady
Slow and Unsteady

D.
Fast and Steady
Fast and Unsteady
Slow and Steady
Slow and Unsteady

5. Mark the picture that best describes the sound you hear. *6*

A.

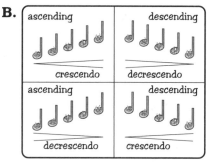

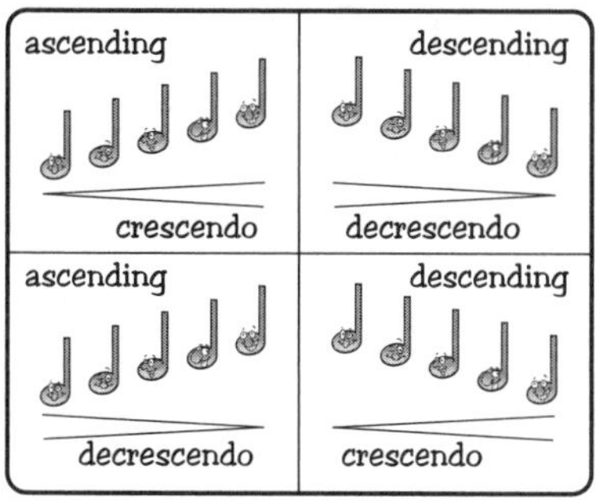

B.

C.

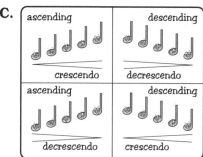

Points

6. Mark the box that best describes the example you hear.   6

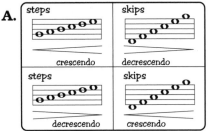
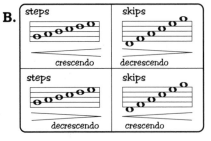
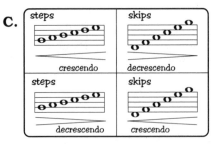

7. Identify the five-finger pattern you hear as Major or minor. Circle your answer.   9

    A. Major   Minor   **B.** Major   Minor   **C.** Major   Minor

8. Identify the 3rd you hear as Major or minor. Circle your answer.   9

    A. Major   Minor   **B.** Major   Minor   **C.** Major   Minor

9. Identify the I (i) chord you hear as Major or minor. Circle your answer.   9

    A. Major   Minor   **B.** Major   Minor   **C.** Major   Minor

10. Identify the interval you hear by circling the correct answer.   8

    A. P1 M2 M3   **B.** M3 M6 P8   **C.** M2 M3 P5   **D.** M2 M3 M7

    E. M2 P4 P5   **F.** P5 M6 P8   **G.** P1 M2 P5   **H.** P5 M7 P8

11. You will hear two rhythms. Determine if the second rhythm is the same or different. Circle the second rhythm that you heard.   8

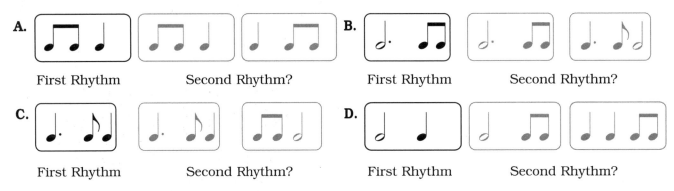

12. Circle the rhythm you hear.   8

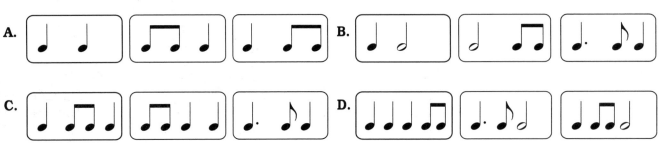

13. As you listen to the rhythm, follow along by counting out loud and pointing to each eighth note. When you hear a note played, draw a line through the eighth note you are pointing to. Draw note values to match the rhythm you marked.   5

Keyboard Gymnastics®

Ear Training Test
Level T1
(Accelerando 1)
Form A

Name _____ **K E Y** _____ Date _____ Score _____ /100 *Points*

1. Circle whether the pitches are the **same** or **different**.   *8*

A. (Same)   Different   B. Same   (Different)

C. Same   (Different)   D. (Same)   Different

2. Circle whether the melodies sound the **same** or **different**.   *8*

A. (Same)   Different   B. (Same)   Different

C. Same   (Different)   D. Same   (Different)

3. Mark the two boxes that best describe the example you hear.   *8*

A.
(High)	(Loud)
Low	Soft

B.
High	(Loud)
(Low)	Soft

C.
(High)	Loud
Low	(Soft)

D.
High	(Loud)
(Low)	Soft

4. Circle the words that best describe the example you hear.   *8*

A. (Fast and Steady)
   Fast and Unsteady
   Slow and Steady
   Slow and Unsteady

B. (Fast and Steady)
   Fast and Unsteady
   Slow and Steady
   Slow and Unsteady

C. Fast and Steady
   (Fast and Unsteady)
   Slow and Steady
   Slow and Unsteady

D. Fast and Steady
   Fast and Unsteady
   Slow and Steady
   (Slow and Unsteady)

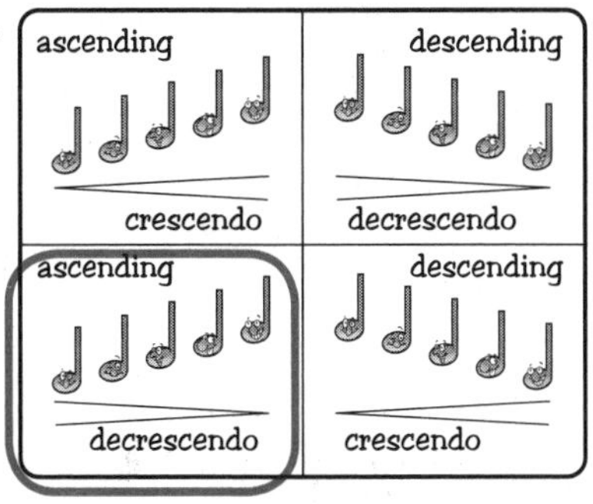

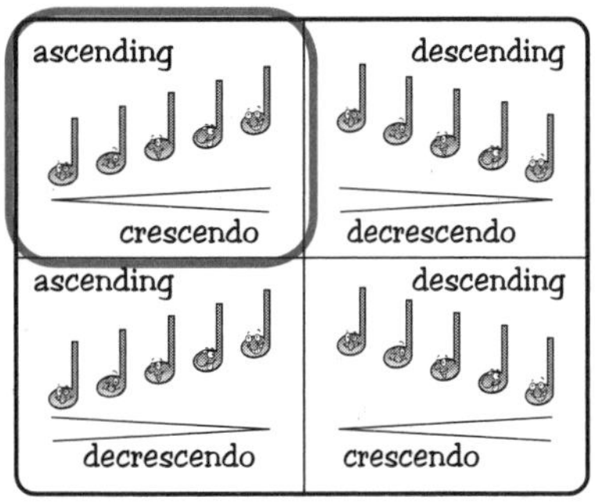

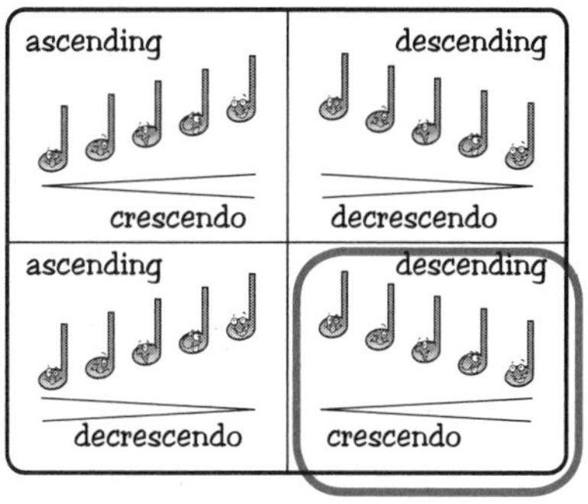

5. Mark the picture that best describes the sound you hear.   *6*

Points

6. Mark the box that best describes the example you hear.   6

A. | steps | skips |
crescendo | decrescendo |
steps | skips |
decrescendo | crescendo |

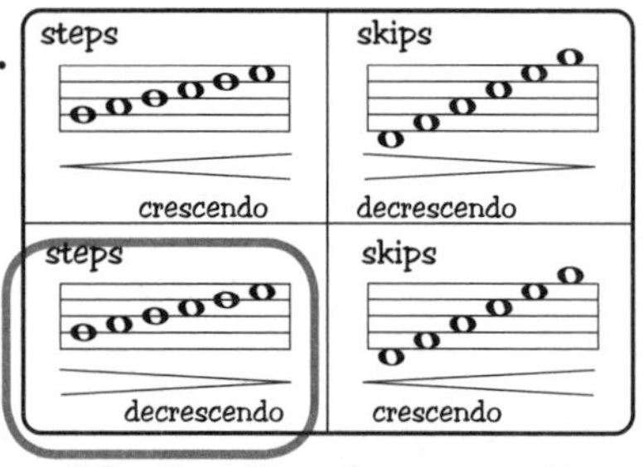

B. | steps | skips |
crescendo | decrescendo |
steps | skips |
decrescendo | crescendo |

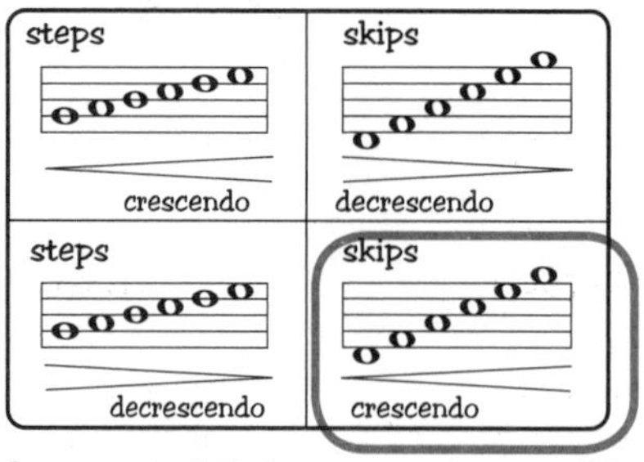

C. | steps | skips |
crescendo | decrescendo |
steps | skips |
decrescendo | crescendo |

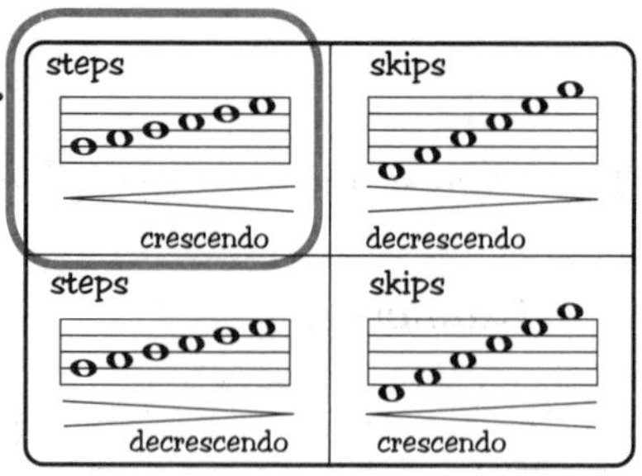

7. Identify the five-finger pattern you hear as Major or minor. Circle your answer.   9

A. Major (Minor)   **B.** Major (Minor)   **C.** (Major) Minor

8. Identify the 3rd you hear as Major or minor. Circle your answer.   9

A. (Major) Minor   **B.** Major (Minor)   **C.** (Major) Minor

9. Identify the I (i) chord you hear as Major or minor. Circle your answer.   9

A. Major (Minor)   **B.** (Major) Minor   **C.** (Major) Minor

10. Identify the interval you hear by circling the correct answer.   8

A. P1 (M2) M3   **B.** (M3) M6 P8   **C.** M2 M3 (P5)   **D.** M2 M3 (M7)

E. M2 (P4) P5   **F.** P5 (M6) P8   **G.** (P1) M2 P5   **H.** P5 (M7) P8

11. You will hear two rhythms. Determine if the second rhythm is the same or different. Circle the second rhythm that you heard.   8

A. First Rhythm   Second Rhythm?   **B.** First Rhythm   Second Rhythm?

C. First Rhythm   Second Rhythm?   **D.** First Rhythm   Second Rhythm?

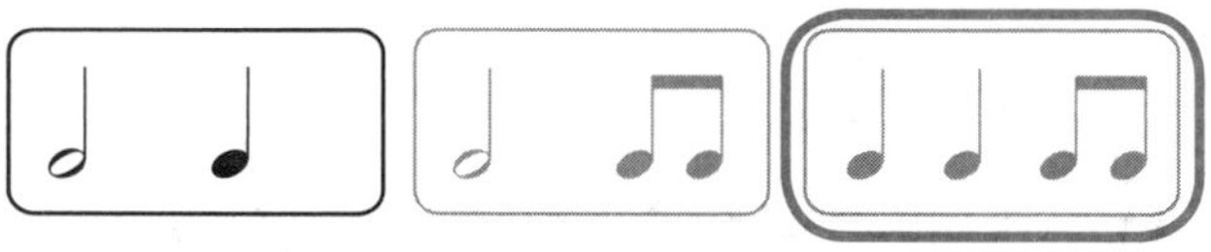

12. Circle the rhythm you hear.   8

A.   **B.**

C.    **D.**

13. As you listen to the rhythm, follow along by counting out loud and pointing to each eighth   5
note. When you hear a note played, draw a line through the eighth note you are pointing
to. Draw note values to match the rhythm you marked.

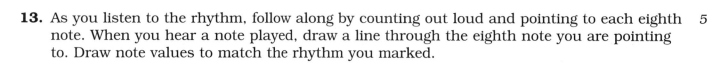

Level T-1 Ear-Training Test Examples

FORM A

Points

1. Circle whether the **pitches** are the same or different.   *8*

2. Circle whether the melodies sound the **same** or **different**.   *8*

3. Mark the two boxes that best describe the example you hear.   *8*

74

Points

8

4. Circle the words that best describe the example you hear.

Example A: Play Fast and Steady

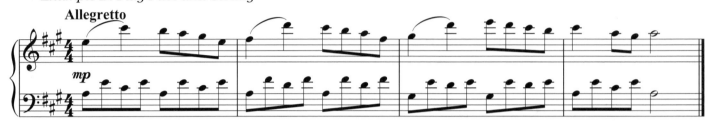

Example B: Play Fast and Steady

Example C: Play Fast and Unsteady

Example D: Play Slow and Unsteady

5. Mark the picture that best describes the sound you hear.

6

Example C

6. Mark the box that best describes the example you hear. 6

Example C

7. Identify the five-finger pattern you hear as **Major** or **minor**. Circle your answer. 9

8. Identify the 3rd you hear as **Major** or **minor**. Circle your answer. 9

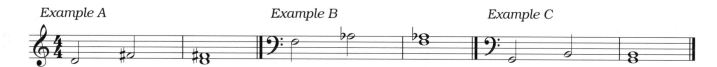

Points

9. Identify the I (i) chord you hear as **Major** or **minor**. Circle your answer.

9

10. Identify the interval you hear by circling the box with the correct answer.

8

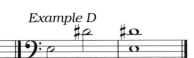

11. You will hear two rhythms. Determine if the second rhythm is the **same** or **different**. Circle the second rhythm that you heard.

8

12. Circle the rhythm you hear.

8

13. Draw note values to match the rhythm you heard and marked.

5

Keyboard Gymnastics®

Name _____ Date _____ Score _____ /100

1. Fill in the missing letters of the music alphabet **moving forward**.   *1*

C __ __ F __ A __ C

2. Fill in the missing letters of the music alphabet **moving backward**.   *1*

G __ B __ D __ __ G   ⟸ START HERE

3. Write the name of each white key on the keyboard.   *1*

4. Write the counts beneath each note and rest in the rhythm below.   *8*

5. Draw the **brace, treble clef sign, double bar, repeat sign, barline,**   *6*
and **bass clef sign** on the grand staff below.

6. Name the notes in the boxes provided.

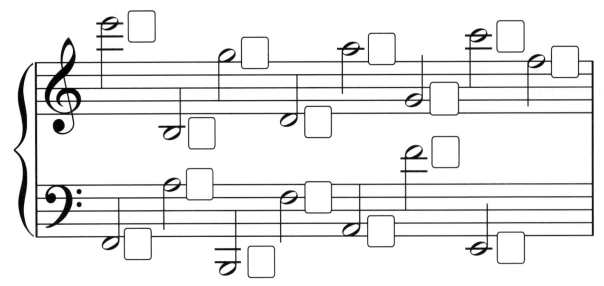

7. Write only one name for each of the shaded keys.

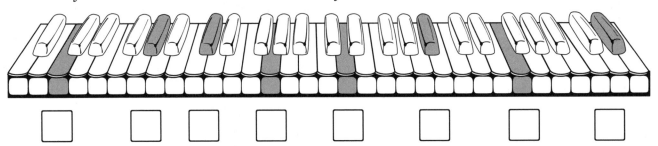

8. Mark the keys on the keyboard to match the notes on the staff. Decide if the notes represent a half step or whole step. **Circle your answer**.

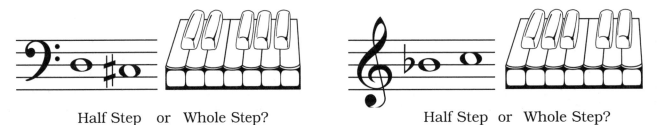

Half Step   or   Whole Step?   Half Step   or   Whole Step?

9. Name the intervals.

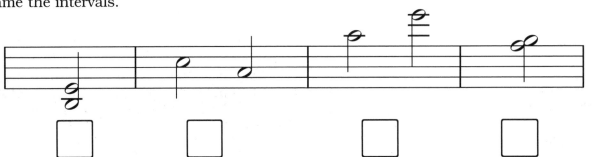

10. True or **False**. Mozart composed more than 600 works in his lifetime.

11. True or **False**. Beethoven could play the violin, viola, organ, and piano.

12. Mark the keys that belong to the **Major five-finger patterns** on the keyboards below.
Using whole notes, draw the five-finger patterns and I chords on the staff.   *12*

| D Major | D Major | DM |
| Five-Finger Pattern | Five-Finger Pattern | I Chord |

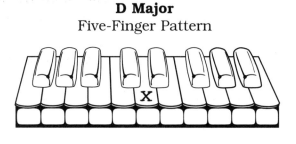
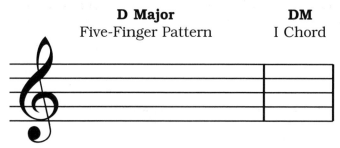

| B♭ Major | B♭ Major | B♭M |
| Five-Finger Pattern | Five-Finger Pattern | I Chord |

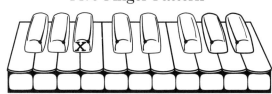
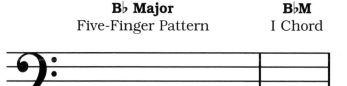

13. Mark the keys that belong to the **minor five-finger patterns** on the keyboards below.
Using whole notes, draw the five-finger patterns and I chords on the staff.   *12*

| E♭ minor | E♭ minor | E♭m |
| Five-Finger Pattern | Five-Finger Pattern | i Chord |

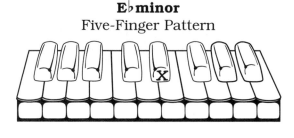
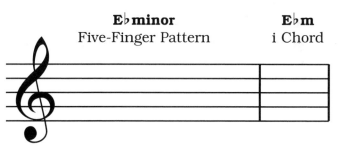

| F minor | F minor | Fm |
| Five-Finger Pattern | Five-Finger Pattern | i Chord |

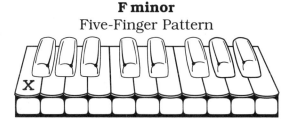
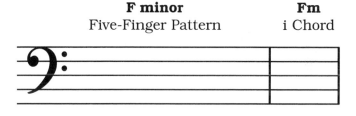

14. Mark the key to complete the 3^{rds}
on the keyboards.   *2*

Up a major 3rd **Down a minor 3rd**

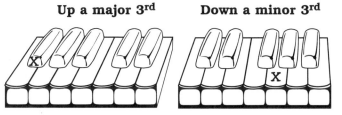

15. Draw the note to complete the 3^{rds}
on the staffs.   *2*

Down a major 3rd **Up a minor 3rd**

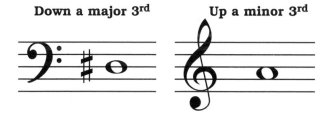

16. Mark the keys to complete the triads
on the keyboards.   *4*

A♭ Major **C♯ minor**

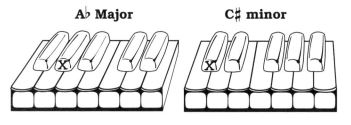

17. Draw the notes to complete the triads
on the staffs.   *4*

F♯ Major **A minor**

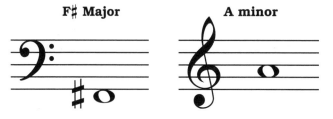

TW201T1

I'm Done Workin' on the Railroad!

Folk/arr. Lloyd

18. There are many things circled in **I'm Done Workin' on the Railroad!** *18*
Find each sign and term listed below and write its number in the box provided.
Write the number of the matching sign by the term in the box provided.

Not all of the circled items will be matched below.

☐ Crescendo	☐ Natural	☐ Dynamic marking means "soft"	☐ A half step
☐ Staccato	☐ Double bar	☐ Term meaning "slow down gradually"	☐ Descending B♭ Major five-finger pattern
☐ Bass clef	☐ Fermata	☐ M3 (Major third)	☐ Repetition
☐ Slur	☐ Decrescendo	☐ Term meaning "walking tempo"	☐ A Flat
☐ Sharp	☐ A half note		

Keyboard Gymnastics®

Name_____ **K E Y** _____ Date_____ Score_____ /100

1. Fill in the missing letters of the music alphabet **moving forward**. *1*

C   D   E   F   G   A   B   C

2. Fill in the missing letters of the music alphabet **moving backward**. *1*

G   A   B   C   D   E   F   G

3. Write the name of each white key on the keyboard. *1*

C D E F G A B

4. Write the counts beneath each note and rest in the rhythm below. *8*

1 + 2 + 3 + 4 +   1 + 2 + 3 + 4 +   1 + 2 + 3 + 4 +   1 + 2 + 3 + 4 +

5. Draw the **brace**, **treble clef sign**, **double bar**, **repeat sign**, **barline**, *6*
and **bass clef sign** on the grand staff below.

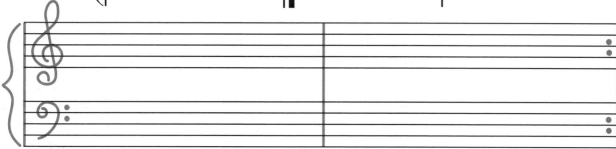

6. Name the notes in the boxes provided. *15*

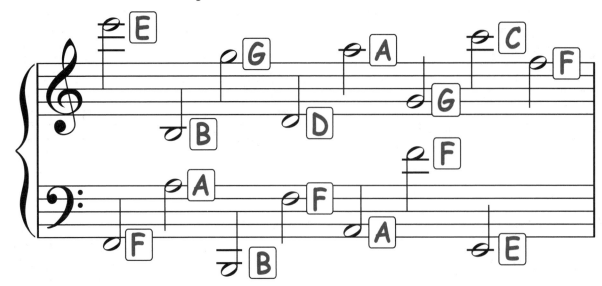

7. Write only one name for each of the shaded keys. *8*

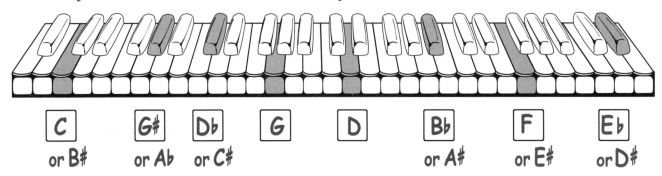

8. Mark the keys on the keyboard to match the notes on the staff. Decide if the notes represent a half step or whole step. **Circle your answer**. *4*

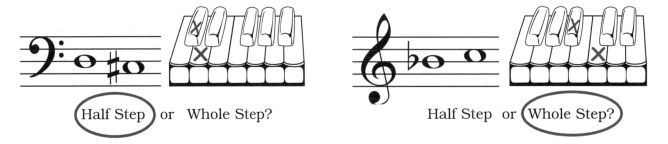

9. Name the intervals. *4*

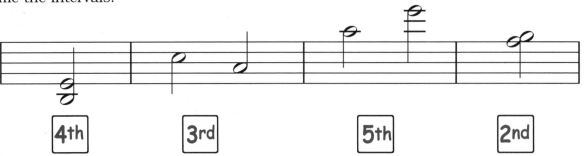

10. **True** or **False**. Mozart composed more than 600 works in his lifetime. *2*

11. **True** or **False**. Beethoven could play the violin, viola, organ, and piano. *2*

12. Mark the keys that belong to the **Major five-finger patterns** on the keyboards below.
Using whole notes, draw the five-finger patterns and I chords on the staff.   *12*

D Major
Five-Finger Pattern

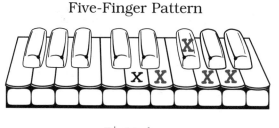

D Major
Five-Finger Pattern

DM
I Chord

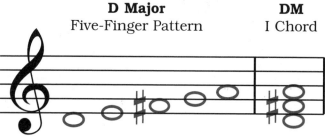

B♭ Major
Five-Finger Pattern

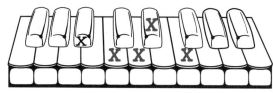

B♭ Major
Five-Finger Pattern

B♭M
I Chord

13. Mark the keys that belong to the **minor five-finger patterns** on the keyboards below.
Using whole notes, draw the five-finger patterns and I chords on the staff.   *12*

E♭ minor
Five-Finger Pattern

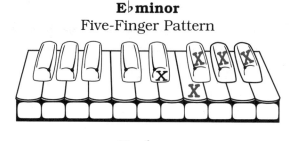

E♭ minor
Five-Finger Pattern

E♭m
i Chord

F minor
Five-Finger Pattern

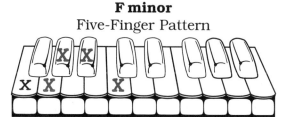

F minor
Five-Finger Pattern

Fm
i Chord

14. Mark the key to complete the 3rds
on the keyboards.   *2*

15. Draw the note to complete the 3rds
on the staffs.   *2*

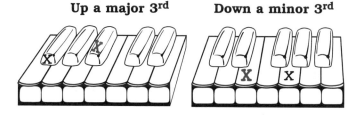

Up a major 3rd   **Down a minor 3rd**   **Down a major 3rd**   **Up a minor 3rd**

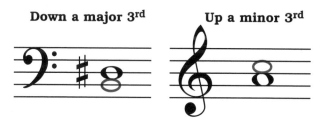

16. Mark the keys to complete the triads
on the keyboards.   *4*

17. Draw the notes to complete the triads
on the staffs.   *4*

A♭ Major   **C♯ minor**   **F♯ Major**   **A minor**

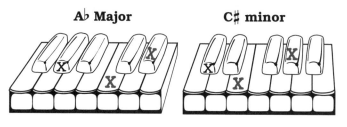
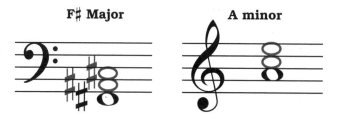

I'm Done Workin' on the Railroad!

Folk/arr. Lloyd

18. There are many things circled in **I'm Done Workin' on the Railroad!**   *18*
Find each sign and term listed below and write its number in the box provided.
Write the number of the matching sign by the term in the box provided.

Not all of the circled items will be matched below.

19 Crescendo	**12** Natural	**15** Dynamic marking means "soft"	**13** A half step
17 Staccato	**25** Double bar	**22** Term meaning "slow down gradually"	**21** Descending B♭ Major five-finger pattern
6 Bass clef	**24** Fermata	**7** M3 (Major third)	**16** Repetition
4 Slur	**23** Decrescendo		
18 Sharp	**14** A half note	**1** Term meaning "walking tempo"	**9** A Flat

Keyboard Gymnastics®

Ear Training Test
Level T1
(Accelerando 1)
Form B

Name_____ Date_____ Score_____ /100   *Points*

1. Circle whether the pitches are the **same** or **different**.   *8*

    A.   Same   Different   **B.**   Same   Different

    C.   Same   Different   **D.**   Same   Different

2. Circle whether the melodies sound the **same** or **different**.   *8*

    A.   Same   Different   **B.**   Same   Different

    C.   Same   Different   **D.**   Same   Different

3. Mark the two boxes that best describe the example you hear.   *8*

A.

High	Loud
Low	Soft

B.

High	Loud
Low	Soft

C.

High	Loud
Low	Soft

D.

High	Loud
Low	Soft

4. Circle the words that best describe the example you hear.   *8*

    A.   Fast and Steady   **B.**   Fast and Steady

        Fast and Unsteady   Fast and Unsteady

        Slow and Steady   Slow and Steady

        Slow and Unsteady   Slow and Unsteady

    C.   Fast and Steady   **D.**   Fast and Steady

        Fast and Unsteady   Fast and Unsteady

        Slow and Steady   Slow and Steady

        Slow and Unsteady   Slow and Unsteady

5. Mark the picture that best describes the sound you hear.   *6*

A.
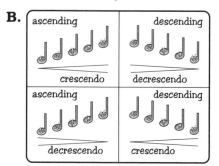

B.
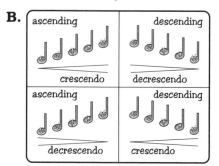

C.
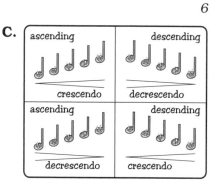

Points

6. Mark the box that best describes the example you hear.   6

A. 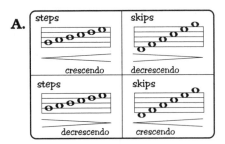 **B.** 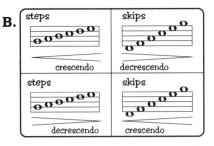 **C.**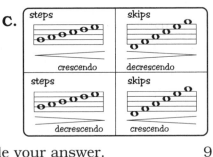

7. Identify the five-finger pattern you hear as Major or minor. Circle your answer.   9

   A.   Major   Minor   **B.**   Major   Minor   **C.**   Major   Minor

8. Identify the 3rd you hear as Major or minor. Circle your answer.   9

   A.   Major   Minor   **B.**   Major   Minor   **C.**   Major   Minor

9. Identify the I (i) chord you hear as Major or minor. Circle your answer.   9

   A.   Major   Minor   **B.**   Major   Minor   **C.**   Major   Minor

10. Identify the interval you hear by circling the correct answer.   8

   A. P1   M2   M6   **B.** P4   M6   P8   **C.** P1   M3   P5   **D.** M2   M7   P8

   E. M3   P4   P8   **F.** M2   P5   P8   **G.** P1   M3   M7   **H.** P4   P5   M6

11. You will hear two rhythms. Determine if the second rhythm is the same or different.
    Circle the second rhythm that you heard.   8

A.    **B.**

First Rhythm   Second Rhythm?   First Rhythm   Second Rhythm?

C.    **D.**

First Rhythm   Second Rhythm?   First Rhythm   Second Rhythm?

12. Circle the rhythm you hear.   8

A.    **B.**

C.    **D.**

13. As you listen to the rhythm, follow along by counting out loud and pointing to each eighth   5
    note. When you hear a note played, draw a line through the eighth note you are pointing
    to. Draw note values to match the rhythm you marked.

Keyboard Gymnastics®

Ear Training Test
Level T1
(Accelerando 1)
Form B
Points

Name_____ **K E Y** _____ Date_____ Score_____ /100

1. Circle whether the pitches are the **same** or **different**. *8*

A. Same (Different) **B.** Same (Different)
C. (Same) Different **D.** Same (Different)

2. Circle whether the melodies sound the **same** or **different**. *8*

A. (Same) Different **B.** Same (Different)
C. Same (Different) **D.** Same (Different)

3. Mark the two boxes that best describe the example you hear. *8*

A.

High	(Loud)
(Low)	Soft

B.

High	Loud
(Low)	(Soft)

C.

High	Loud
(Low)	(Soft)

D.

(High)	(Loud)
Low	Soft

4. Circle the words that best describe the example you hear. *8*

A.
Fast and Steady
Fast and Unsteady
Slow and Steady
(Slow and Unsteady)

B.
(Fast and Steady)
Fast and Unsteady
Slow and Steady
Slow and Unsteady

C.
Fast and Steady
Fast and Unsteady
(Slow and Steady)
Slow and Unsteady

D.
Fast and Steady
(Fast and Unsteady)
Slow and Steady
Slow and Unsteady

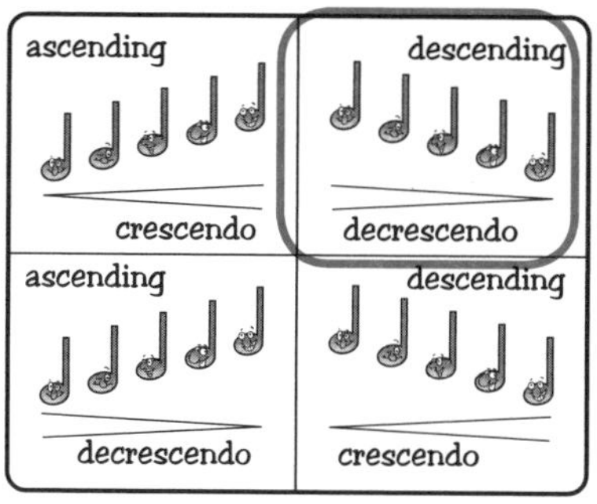

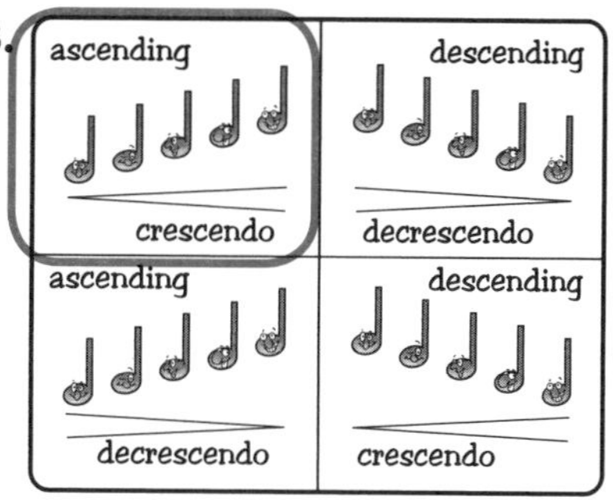

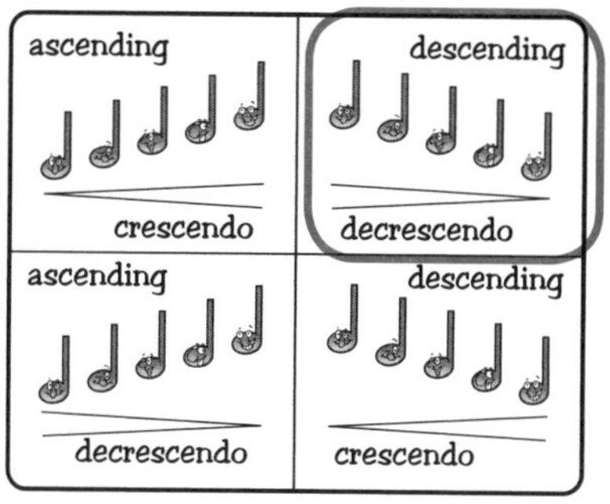

5. Mark the picture that best describes the sound you hear. *6*

Points

6. Mark the box that best describes the example you hear. 6

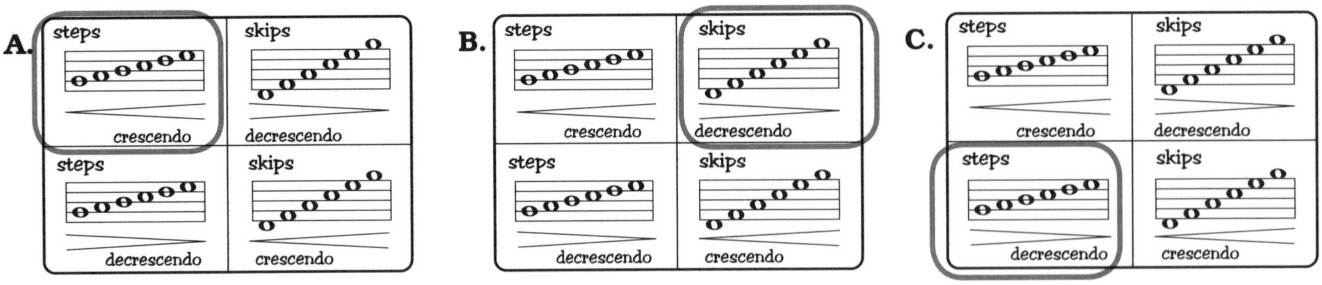

A. | steps | skips |
crescendo | decrescendo |
steps | skips |
decrescendo | crescendo |

B. | steps | skips |
crescendo | decrescendo |
steps | skips |
decrescendo | crescendo |

C. | steps | skips |
crescendo | decrescendo |
steps | skips |
decrescendo | crescendo |

7. Identify the five-finger pattern you hear as Major or minor. Circle your answer. 9

A. (Major)   Minor   **B.** Major (Minor)   **C.** Major (Minor)

8. Identify the 3rd you hear as Major or minor. Circle your answer. 9

A. (Major)   Minor   **B.** Major (Minor)   **C.** Major (Minor)

9. Identify the I (i) chord you hear as Major or minor. Circle your answer. 9

A. Major (Minor)   **B.** (Major) Minor   **C.** Major (Minor)

10. Identify the interval you hear by circling the correct answer. 8

A. P1 M2 (M6)   **B.** (P4) M6 P8   **C.** (P1) M3 P5   **D.** M2 M7 (P8)

E. (M3) P4 P8   **F.** M2 (P5) P8   **G.** P1 M3 (M7)   **H.** P4 P5 (M6)

11. You will hear two rhythms. Determine if the second rhythm is the same or different.
Circle the second rhythm that you heard. 8

A.  First Rhythm   Second Rhythm?   **B.**  First Rhythm   Second Rhythm?

C. 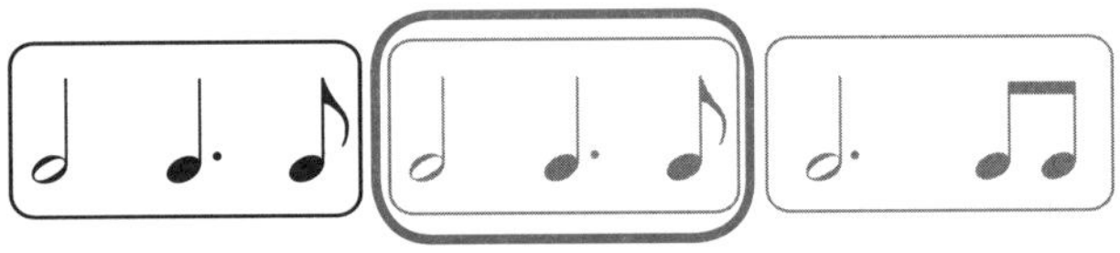 First Rhythm   Second Rhythm?   **D.**  First Rhythm   Second Rhythm?

12. Circle the rhythm you hear. 8

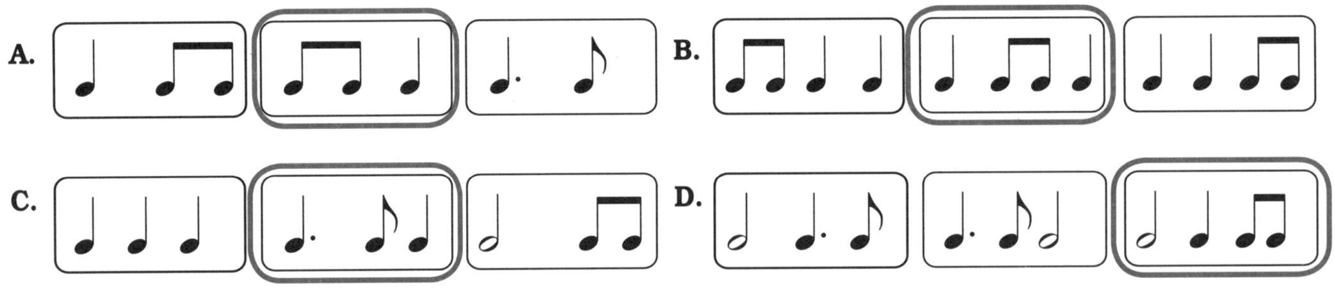

A.   **B.**

C.   **D.**

13. As you listen to the rhythm, follow along by counting out loud and pointing to each eighth 5
note. When you hear a note played, draw a line through the eighth note you are pointing
to. Draw note values to match the rhythm you marked.

Level T-1 Ear-Training Test Examples

FORM B

Points

1. Circle whether the pitches are the **same** or **different**. *8*

Example A *Example B* *Example C* *Example D*

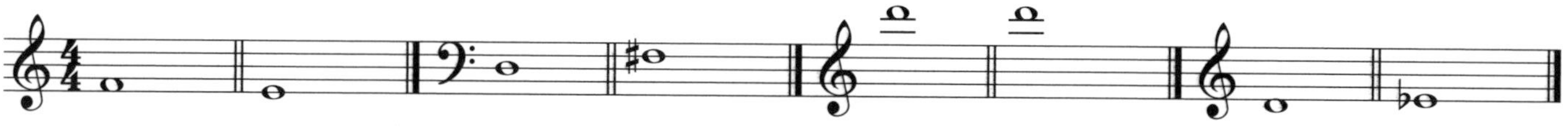

2. Circle whether the melodies sound the **same** or **different.** *8*

A. *Melody 1* *Melody 2*

Moderato

3
f
pause

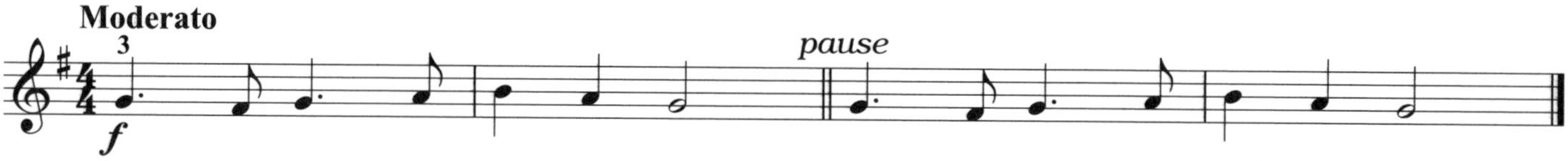

B. *Melody 1* *Melody 2*

Allegro

pause
mp
2

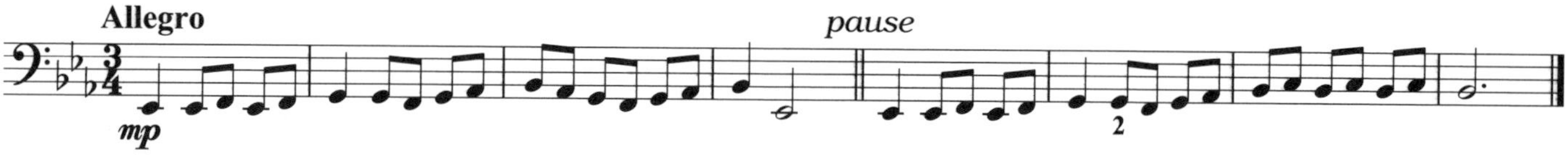

C. *Melody 1* *Melody 2*

Allegretto

pause
mf

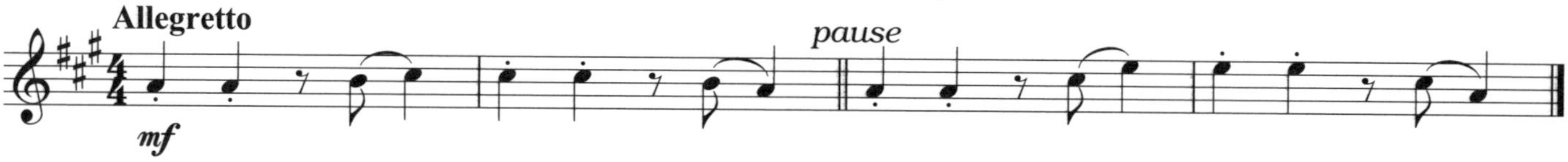

D. *Melody 1* *Melody 2*

Andante

pause
mp

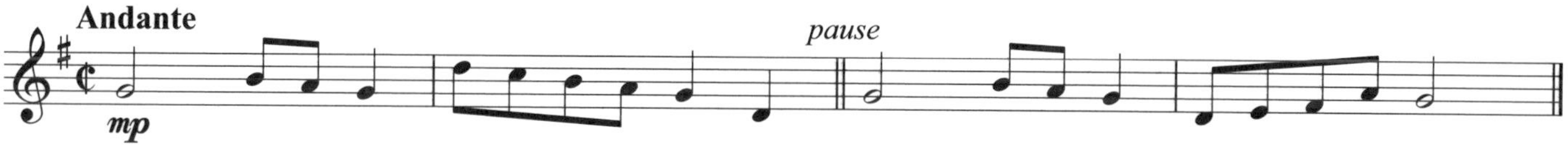

3. Mark the two boxes that best describe the example you hear. *8*

Example A *Example B*

Vivace **Adagio**

ff
pp

Example C *Example D*

Largo **Andante**

8va
p
8vb
ff

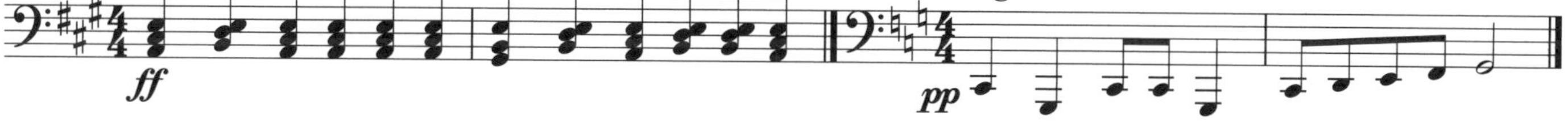

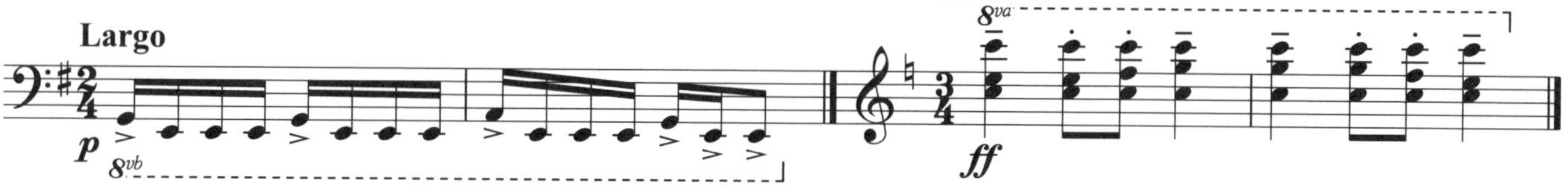

4. Circle the words that best describe the example you hear.

8

Example A: Play Slow and Unsteady

Example B: Play Fast and Steady

Example C: Play Slow and Steady

Example D: Play Fast and Unsteady

5. Mark the picture that best describes the sound you hear.

6

Example A *Example B*

Example C

6. Mark the box that best describes the example you hear. 6

Example C

7. Identify the five-finger pattern you hear as **Major** or **minor**. Circle your answer. 9

8. Identify the 3rd you hear as **Major** or **minor**. Circle your answer. 9

9. Identify the I (i) chord you hear as **Major** or **minor**. Circle your answer.   9

Example A   *Example B*   *Example C*

10. Identify the interval you hear by circling the box with the correct answer.   8

Example A   *Example B*   *Example C*   *Example D*

Example E   *Example F*   *Example G*   *Example H*

11. You will hear two rhythms. Determine if the second rhythm is the **same** or **different**.   8
Circle the second rhythm that you heard.

Example A   *Example B*   *Example C*   *Example D*

12. Circle the rhythm you hear.   8

Example A   *Example B*   *Example C*   *Example D*

13. Draw note values to match the rhythm you heard and marked.   5